LLEWELLYN'S
2006
WICCA
ALMANAC

Featuring

Sheela Ardrian, Elizabeth Barrette, Chandra Beal,
Phillip Bernhardt-House, Boudica, Jennifer Cobb,
Emely Flak, Karen Glasgow-Follett, Sharynne
NicMhacha, Christopher Penczak, Diana Rajchel, Flame
Ravenhawk, Steven Repko, Cerridwen Iris Shea,
Norman Shoaf, Tammy Sullivan

Llewellyn's 2006 Wicca Almanac

ISBN 0-7387-0309-5. Copyright by Llewellyn Publications, Woodbury, Minnesota, USA. All rights reserved.

Printed in the United States of America on recycled paper.

Editor/Designer: Michael Fallon

Cover Designer: Gavin Dayton Duffy

Cover Images: © Digital Vision; © BrandX Pictures; © Digital Stock; © Photodisc; © Comstock; © Thinkstock

Interior Illustrations: Selina Alko 19, 23, 197, 199, 267, 270; Christiane Grauert 29, 33, 72, 76, 256, 261, 263; Matt Kenyon 39, 105, 108, 110; Terry Miura 94, 97, 236, 240; Brian Raszka 8, 12, 50, 56, 205, 247, 250; Stephen Schildbach 215, 219; Keri Smith 66, 85, 88, 183, 187; Richard Wehrman 227, 279

Additional Clip Art Illustrations: © PhotoDisc; © Brand X Pictures; © Digital Stock; © Corbis; © Thinkstock; © Comstock; © Art Explosion. Models are used for illustrative purposes only.

Special thanks to Amber Wolfe for the use of daily color correspondences. For more detailed information on this subject, please see *Personal Alchemy* by Amber Wolfe.

You can order Llewellyn annuals and books from *New Worlds,* Llewellyn's magazine catalog. To request a free copy of the catalog, call toll-free 1-877-NEW-WRLD, or visit our website at http://subscriptions.llewellyn.com.

Astrological calculations are performed by the Kepler 6.1 astrology software program, specially created for Llewellyn Publications, and with the kind permission of Cosmic Patterns Software, Inc., www.AstroSoftware.com

Llewellyn Worldwide
Dept. 0-7387-0309-5
2143 Wooddale Drive
Woodbury, MN 55125-2989

www.llewellyn.com

Llewellyn's 2006 Wicca Almanac

Contents

Almanac Section: Spring 2006 to Spring 2007

*The days & the nights, the Moon & the stars, the colors & the energies,
& all the latest Wiccan/Pagan news—the yearly almanac gives you everything
you need to get you through this heady astrological year*

Chapter Four: Over the Cauldron

*Up-to-date Wiccan opinions & rantings
overheard & spelled out just for you*

Chapter Five: God Said, Goddess Said

*A lively discussion between the sexes,
about the sexes, & occasionally about sex*

Chapter Six: The Virtual Witch

The Wicca wide web, technology, buying-selling, & electronic magic

Introduction

Welcome, readers, to the latest edition of Llewellyn's *Wicca Almanac*. It's a funny culture, isn't it? So much happening all the time, an absolutely overwhelming number of choices, too much to do and too little time. I was in the supermarket the other day, and I counted twenty-three different varieties just of diet cola (diet *cola!*). There's lemon diet cola, cherry diet cola, lime diet cola, diet cola with sugar substitute, diet cola with sugar derivative, and on and on (into infinity).

In the midst of all the daily chaos, is it any wonder many people today slog through the day without hardly bothering to pause and consider what's the point of it all? It's a wonder any of us can get from morning to night, as deluged as we all are.

Well, congrats to you, for pausing a moment to look at the *Wicca Almanac*. This book is a collection of the best and latest thinking about how to decipher this indecipherable world. Check out page 64, for instance, for tips on how to keep a sanity-inducing, Pagan-oriented journal. Or maybe you'll find solace from the article on page 192, which has tips on how to negotiate the confusing medical system in modern-day America. All through this edition, along with yearly calendar and holiday information, you will find in-depth and opinionated articles on current fashions, on Pagan art and music, on Wiccans and Witches in the media, on travel, on modern-day sexuality, and so on—all written by writers willing to face the confusion of modern life head-on. The *Wicca Almanac* is geared to the do-it-yourself aesthetic, to young practitioners of the world's most ancient spiritual traditions who are working to make sense of the world.

Lifestyles of the Witch & Famous

Wiccan & Pagan fashions
& lifestyles, media sightings,
gossip & tidbits, & all things
wicked & Witchy

Harnessing the Spirit of the City

by Diana Rajchel

I grew up in Indiana near Chicago during the 1980s and 1990s. My hometown was cut off from its Hoosier roots, as the news from Chicago dominated our area. The problem was so pronounced that people I grew up with still say "Chicago" when asked where they are from.

I thought this location schizophrenia a hilarious thing, and I think of the place of my birth as a city that thought it was a town that thought it was a city. Ah, Crown Point and its poor, misguided residents— they were too rural for the big leagues, and too urban for its Indiana basketball-loving neighbors. Crown Point was alone in its

county, completely misunderstood by all on both sides of the rural/urban divide.

As an adult, I feel a touch of guilt for mocking my hometown. For all the misguided pretensions of its residents, my town gave me a firm spiritual support in the face of the social derision I experienced growing up there. Even when pelted with taunts about the clothing I sewed myself, about my dad's shifting professions, or about just my character, I knew on an unconscious level that the spirit of my city liked me more than it appreciated the herds of snotty interlopers spitting on its central square.

I never descended into depression or despair despite my unpleasant childhood; I think because I always felt connected to place I lived even if I didn't connect with my neighbors. A favorable city spirit gives support and love and will do its best to drive off those who would harm anyone under its care. Whenever enough individuals cluster on one patch of land, a spirit will tend to form there that can alter the original aura and mood of that very environment.

Some city spirits, of course, do not tend their inhabitants with quite so much care. I never did get along with Chicago, for example—in part because my mother prefers to avoid dense populations and passed this claustrophobia on to me. Learning how to drive amidst the commuter traffic of northwest Indiana also did nothing to encourage in me any affection toward the big city.

Just as all past relationships can, if left unchecked, haunt the present, my past relationship with Chicago gave me a rocky start with my new home—the Twin Cities. When I began to acquaint myself with Minneapolis and Saint Paul, it came about as an exercise in resetting boundaries.

The Spirit of My Current City Home

The spirit of my current city is ever-shifting and changing. As the economy and transportation methods have changed within the city, as new immigrant populations and social activists have become compelling social forces, the very spirit of Minneapolis has changed its shape and gender. The tough Scandinavian spirit that dominated Minnesota early in its history has faded as the Scandinavians have left for more rural areas. Now, as people take a train to work, as the economy changes to service and finance jobs, and as new populations from Somalia, India, and Latin America form their own neighborhoods, the appearance of the city spirit has altered.

Today, instead of a white, Nordic, male warehouse worker, my city's spirit is a fashionably dressed woman with a dark tan whose shoes are a little less than fashionable. She is urban, technologically savvy, and wholly with-it. She values status and smiles upon urban renewal as yet another way to honor and beautify herself. She is just a little bit corrupt, but more in the pell-mell fashion of a young woman on the make rather than a greedy old crone.

This is the spirit that I neglected to introduce myself properly to upon moving into the Warehouse District of Minneapolis, not far from the city's heart at Loring Park. Upon reading *Urban Primitive* and taking a good look at the streets I was walking every day, I realized my mistake: I was not making an effort to get to know this city spirit, so I was not yet part of the bustling mass of people filling the streets of downtown with endless energy.

Whenever enough individuals cluster on one patch of land, a spirit will tend to form there.

For a good time, I kept my energy apart and did not create a home to shield myself from the buzzing urban energy. My sustenance, home, and life were thus in constant struggle. Only after some time did it occur to me that perhaps I needed to tend to some formalities: just as the ancient Egyptians expected an acknowledgement of their local gods, I needed to pay homage to my own city spirit hovering above and below the nearby park and buildings and streets.

How to Connect with a City Spirit

The gods that watched me presented hints on how to approach my city spirit, but I wasn't paying attention. I happened to befriend a man who could have been a priest to the temple of Minneapolis, if he only was aware of such things. He worships this city and loves its spirit that much. When we walk through downtown together he stops, always beguiled by the fine shape of the I.D.S. Tower. He complains bitterly how buildings have streets stolen from the city in the name of a highway to get to (oh the profanity!) the suburbs. He loves that the police force as a collective isn't quite sane, and that the graffiti often includes political and mathematical jokes. His tours with me of museums and of the downtown district helped me find my way and finally feel comfortable. When we parted ways, I had the same love and appreciation for Minneapolis as he did.

After eighteen months of living in the city, long after my departure from this urban priest, I introduced myself to the city spirit. One summer evening I trekked to Loring Park, and the goddesses Squat and Skor smiled upon my efforts. I arrived at a single vacated parking space just after the time that meters were no longer monitored. I walked around the park until I found a good, comfortable view of tall buildings on one side of downtown, and made my introduction.

Invocation to the Spirit of the City

I open my heart to the spirit of the city,
Minneapolis.
You who embrace the mighty Mississippi,
I bring myself to you, city spirit,
I come now to your heart.
I hear your music,
The thunder of your river,
The stillness of your lakes.

I dive into the give-and-take of the city,
I make myself known.
I am (state your name),
I am a new Witch to this city.

I knock upon your door and ask your admission,
Spirit of the city,
I work here, I live here.
Show me what can make me well;
I open my mind to your voice, that you may tell.
Spirit of the city of Minneapolis,
What's going on?

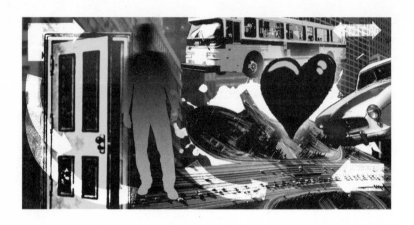

As I opened my mind in meditation, I entreated her energy to come to me. Immediately, I felt as thought I had touched upon a tornado equipped with strobe lights. Thoughts, images, and concepts flashed through my mind. If I focused enough on one corner of the noise, I felt I zoomed in on an individual apartment. In one spot, I could hear keys clicking on a keyboard; in another I felt the wind running through the corridors between the city's tall buildings, and I could sense a great, wafting power being generated from one of the dance clubs downtown.

I pulled back into myself enough to retain a sense of being "other" and "apart" from the city, and I asked the spirit the question recommended by the authors of *Urban Primitive:* "What's going on?"

The answer I received was: "Life! I am crawling with life!"

Thus, I engaged in my first true dialogue with the spirit of Minneapolis. She had wondered about me—coming into her city and tapping the land for magic without making a proper introduction. I made a sincere apology, and told her I never like it when new neighbors trespass upon me. But when they ask to borrow a cup of flour rather than marching into my kitchen and taking it, I always enjoy the opportunity to share.

I worked hard to make up for the a similar faux pas I had made with Minneapolis by treating her as just a collection of buildings and streets rather than as a city empowered by the spirit that hovers within it.

Maintaining a City Spirit Relationship

Since those days after I made amends, I've made visits to Minneapolis's "temples" and brought friends—fellow urban Witches like me who also needed a proper acquaintance with the city spirit. We take the train to city hall, and I often open with this guided meditation.

City Spirit Guided Meditation

Listen to the sounds around you—
The buzz of traffic, voices down streets.
Movement of machines and buildings.

Turn your attention to the sidewalk,
and what goes on below each building.
What life acts out its dramas beneath your feet
every single day?

Pick a building in front of you,
and reach high up with your mind.
Enter through a window—it doesn't matter how.
Walk across the floor.
Peer in stairwells.
Punch the elevator buttons.
Think: Who else comes here every day?
What is their daily routine? How do they get here?
When do they eat, where do they go? What do they eat?
How do they leave?

Look into the sky above the buildings.
What goes through the sky every day?
Pretend you are a wave of sound—
A radio signal, a television signal,
bouncing off walls and hurtling through sky.

Some of you end at an airplane, others, an antenna,
A few land at last in the grass and sink.

Look at the road in front of you—
The cars that travel it every day.
Think about the stories contained
In each and every passing car,
Stories that bring them to this part of the street—
some only once, some every single day.

Now stop, and ground and center yourself.
Think about the city around you,
And just be in it.
What is your place in this creature?

At the end of this guided meditation, I walk up to the doors of city hall, knock on the door three times, and leave a gold coin. In my inner ear, I hear the approving buzz and hum of the city and feel approval from Athena.

The city hall is the closest thing modern U.S. cities have to a temple. Here is where people come perhaps once in their lives, or perhaps over and over again, to meet the demands of the society and the city where they live. People petition the city council as other cultures might have petitioned tribal elders. Punishments, rewards, and celebrations are decided within the walls of the city hall. The Minneapolis City Hall building emits so much energy that its four stories seem on par with the twenty-plus story buildings sharing its neighborhood. The people who spend a lot of time in this building at night or during the day ultimately do it for the love of it, for the beauty of the architecture, or for their belief in local government and their belief in the city of Minneapolis.

I find the force of city energy overpowering at times, and I approach with caution even as the familiarity between me and the city spirit builds. Any interaction that invites too much energy into my body can trigger an extreme nervous reaction, while the noise brought by true contact with the city spirit can enervate me or lead me into a state of overanxiety. Especially when I first moved to Minneapolis, I had to wear hematite jewelry every day, and even now I must take special care to ground and center several times while I am out on the town.

The city spirit forms from the movement of millions of people, from literal and figurative wheels turning, from violence, kindness, and bustle distributed throughout the neighborhoods. A simple shield can protect against each of these when encountered face to face, but when it hovers around you like humid air—as it is prone to do in the compressed space of a city—shields need constant reinforcement and empathic talents need grounding.

> I take all the opportunities I can to dialogue with my city now—waiting for train or bus, or just sitting outside.

I take all the opportunities I can to dialogue with my city now—when I wait for a train or bus, when I sit outside, when I am at home I chat with the spirit. While hunting for a job I made a special journey, meditating upon the city, and left an offering of a small daisy and the Norse rune for prosperity in chalk upon the city steps. I continue to meditate upon the city and to chat with her, asking for help so that I can provide for myself and live comfortably within her city limits. The city speaks to me by the buzzing of energy I feel when I approach the heart of its buildings and move through its city streets.

Serendipity and chance often are how the city spirit guides me. I may suddenly see a sign for a shop that's hiring that I'd never noticed before, or feel an inclination to turn a different direction and encounter a friend I haven't seen in an age. When I needed an oasis from a difficult temp job, I felt a need to go just a few feet farther in the skyway and found an odd corner building with a privately owned coffee shop in a very quiet space. For some reason, even though I don't live there, the city directs me frequently to the University of Minnesota neighborhood, where I run into friends from the city or even from other places I've lived.

It's a cooperative relationship. I have agreed to become part of the city organism, and thus the city allows me to tap into its spinning vortex for my workings. Or else the city directs messages to me of danger or interest as though I am a limb and the spirit has the brain.

Even now I am carving a relationship with Minneapolis. When I was still in the Warehouse District, she kept flashing images of me sitting on the steps of my building, cigarette in hand, telling her of my day. She seems to like it when I bring visitors to her temple. Minneapolis has a lot to say to me and to teach me. I already know what she wants in return is for me to create—to write, and, thus, to feed her spirit with the offering of my talents.

This is my city that has allowed me a place within its heart. Speak of your city, know your land, and experience what it means to live as part of a heartbeat. There is much magic to be made, and much creation to begin.

Erotic Wicca

by Tammy Sullivan

Ah, those marvelous moments when we can give ourselves over to the sensual side of life. One can't help but welcome an interlude with the erotic when one has the chance, as it reminds us how wonderfully alive we are. Contact with erotic energy may only be a brief moment out of a very busy day—perhaps a small fantasy or a memory of a special time with a loved one—but any contact energizes the soul.

Throughout history, Pagans have enjoyed these energies and have celebrated them with rituals such as the Great Rite and festivals of free sexuality. The ancient Roman festival of Floralia was a yearly event held in honor of the goddess Flora. This particular festival was well-known for its wanton sexuality—even marriage vows were suspended for the duration of the festivities.

Granted, we aren't prone to such public spectacles today, and many of us prefer that a spiritual connection exists between our partners and ourselves, but Pagans as a rule are more open minded than others about fleshly pleasures. Whereas society dictates that the "normal" sexual union is a heterosexual bond between two people that is meant to be forever, Paganism takes a more balanced approach.

Eroticism reminds us how wonderfully alive we are.

Pagan Sexual Mores

The first step toward a Pagan joining is the handfasting, which is a year-and-a-day trial marriage. Sexual preference does not matter in this ceremony, and in fact some handfastings are group events. At the end of the handfasting period, the participants may decide to renew their vows and be forever joined through this life and any others. It is through such openness that the vibrations of love and spirit come through to manifest into our lives on a positive level.

Even so, when dealing with such a personal, and sometimes tricky, topic as eroticism combined with religion or spirituality there is one key subject that must be addressed—ethics. Let's get it out of the way first.

A path that is considered spiritual in nature has no room for preconceived notions or prejudices. It does not matter what type of chromosome you carry or what gender you are attracted to any more than it would matter what color your hair is. The aim is to relate to the spirit of the person, not only the body. Spirit is color- and gender-blind; it is who we are under the skin that matters in spirit.

As Wiccans or Pagans, our role is to observe and accept the choices of others, not to place ourselves in a seat where we can render false judgments on someone's character based upon their

sexual preferences or any other fleshly trait. We are above none, we are all one.

Pagans generally view erotic energy as natural and healthy. Sex is nothing to feel guilty about; it is a celebration of life, the very act that perpetuates the human race. Personal choices come into play when one is considering one's own ethical stance toward erotic energy within everyday life. However, there is one ethic that must stand firm no matter what type of energy one is working with: "Harm none." Within this simple two-word statement, all questions are answered. Moreover, in sex you must be honest and forthcoming about any possibility of harm you may cause (however inadvertently). Also, your safety is ultimately your responsibility, and while I know it goes against the natural instinct you must use protection. You are risking great harm to yourself and future partners otherwise.

"Harm none" relates to all acts of eroticism that are consensual and to all participants of legal age and sound mind at the time. I must clarify this a bit further. If your path is shamanistic in nature and you wish to have relations while under the influence, it is your right to do so. However, never take for granted that another will feel the same way about it. Many Witches like to keep their systems pure, and that is their choice. Many Witches also do not wish to have relations with someone who is under the influence of any intoxicating substance. Please be honest about any drug use and about your state of mind.

Just as it is okay to be sexual, for Pagans it is also okay to be celibate. There is a large accounting in history that speaks of sacred celibacy, as well as sacred prostitution. The vestal virgins, the forerunners to today's Catholic nuns, are perhaps the best-known Pagan group of celibate females, but they are far from the only ones. Even if celibate, you can still put erotic energy to work through magical means if you choose.

Magical Sexuality

The priestesses that served Aphrodite were expected to ritually engage in sexual activities with those that visited her temple. These priestesses were highly respected. A man would enter the temple as a personification of the horned one, and the priestess would take on the role of the goddess incarnate. The union was viewed as a way to honor deity and the life force. It was considered a sacred duty.

Whatever path you choose—be it temple whore or vestal virgin—Paganism has room for all. According to Hesiod, the Greek god Eros (the root of the word "erotic") was one of the three primordial beings along with Chaos and Gaia. He was known to the Romans as both Cupid and Amor and was portrayed as a handsome youth with wings. He was honored as the god of love, sex, and sensual pleasures. When he kisses Psyche and wakes her from her sleep, we find not only the

Magical practitioners have long manipulated erotic energies in spell work, captivating mind and body.

inspiration for a popular children's fairy tale but also a metaphor for the energizing effect of erotic energy. Erotic vibrations are at the roots of our species; they are part of our instinct. They vibrate in us at the deepest level. Erotic energy has been responsible for inspiring everything from works of art to war.

Erotic energy weaves a tangible web throughout the historical mythos spanning all cultures. From Pele to Xochiquetzal to Aphrodite, we envision a world of seduction in our legends. It is a magical feeling indeed to know that you, through your erotic spirit, are sharing the same vibrations with tantalizing gods and goddesses throughout the ages.

Manipulating Erotic Energies

Magical practitioners have long manipulated erotic energies in spell work; they captivate both mind and body. Eastern traditions make use of tao and tantra to bring the body to bliss and the spirit closer to the divine. It is believed that these practices will align and clean the chakras, and balance yin and yang energy—thereby increasing overall good health.

Erotic Vibrations

To make use of traditional magical methods for rituals or spell work, we must first understand this type of vibration. Erotic energy usually presents itself with at least one of the following characteristics: an overall feeling of warmth, a slight red or pink flushing of the skin, slightly unstable breathing, a feeling of heady or humid air or an electric jolt or slow throbbing in the pelvic region.

These sensations can hit you like lightning and then, just as quickly, flee completely. They have been likened to a serpent coiled in the base of the spine preparing to strike. Erotic energy causes a slow building of tension and desire. We release the energy when the desire is the strongest.

Controlling Passion

Passion has been known to go wild of its own accord. It is a thin line that we walk when working with such a volatile energy as passion, and it's best to keep that in mind. Desire can also easily confuse the conjuror, so maintaining clarity is essential for practicing successful passion magic. A rubber band placed around the wrist can help if you remember to snap it when your mind drifts too far from your goal.

Historically, magical workers could conjure and banish erotic energy, focus power toward a goal, or use it as a sort of astral gateway. This may be done alone or with a partner. It is a simple task of allowing your imagination to go wherever it wants until a strong desire is present. Once you feel you have reached the highest point that you can, focus your attention on the goal at hand and hold it in your mind as long as possible before the final release.

Aphrodisiac Magic

Aphrodisiacs have always been part of the Witch's bag of tricks. Some recipes were closely guarded, while others were placed in plain view. A magical powder, for instance, would be hidden, but placing a bouquet of red roses in the open serves the same purpose and there is no need to be subversive about it. Hiding your intentions can be manipulative but can also be harmless under certain conditions. Some aphrodisiacs, such as raw oysters, pasta, chocolate, and coffee are downright delicious. Serving a loved one a wonderful dinner is not manipulative nor harmful but instead quite a treat.

Likewise, a favorite scent may produce desire in another person when you wear it; this is also not harmful. In fact, when used as scented massage oil it can be quite stimulating. After all, who doesn't like a massage?

Erotic Aromas and Sensations

You can boost erotic vibrations around the home with heady aromas like sandalwood, candlelight, or rich sensuous colors and textures. Replace your cotton sheets with sheets of satin. Scent the linens in the wash cycle with a lavender rinse. Hoyas, passion plants, and jasmine vines create haunting fragrances that waft through each room. Make your home an erotic journey for each of the senses.

Basic Tips for Erotic Magic

When using erotic energy as the source power for magic in ritual, preparation is key. Erotic energy builds at a fast rate. Involving all five senses will help it make a slower, steadier climb. If you use a simple precleansing routine, for this type of work you will want to jazz it up. Light candles and incense to add ambiance. Play relaxing music in the background. Sip a glass of wine or juice. After all, this is a seduction scene.

If you shower, wash with your hands instead of with a cloth, and use slow, languorous strokes. If you bathe, allow yourself to soak for awhile in the warm water. Rub scented oil into your skin, and then blot dry gently. Stretch out. If you practice yoga do a few postures to get the blood flowing. If you

don't, simple warm-up stretches will work fine. You may decide to make up your face to add glamour, it is also fine to go *au naturel*. Using whatever helps one build the tension slowly is always the correct choice.

It is always best to plan for this type of ritual to be performed skyclad (nude). This is both for practical reasons and to keep the energy at its highest point. After all, nothing is more erotic than candlelight dancing on smooth, naked skin.

Once you have sufficiently warmed your body with mild exercises, you may cast your circle and begin the ritual.

Place items that both honor the elements and invite erotic energy to the altar. Perfect examples are a feather for air, ice for water, a candle for fire, and a rich chocolate candy for earth. These items will work double duty as they can be employed in the ritual as well as paying tribute to and honoring the elements.

When it comes to food, the old ways are best—perhaps because in the past there was so little to entertain us that food was a more central focus.

Remember as you progress that this is a completely personal ritual, so if it feels right then it is right. There is no wrong way. You may wish to pull the energy along the chakra path all the way to the third eye before release, as this is supposed to to make for an easier release when it comes to magical tasks. Or it might be that you have a unique way of releasing the energy on your own for magic; just do whatever feels right. Maintaining your focus may be a little tough, but that should be your only obstacle. Tailor your words, the colors you use, incense, and so on to suit only yourself and what turns you on. Or else you may choose to follow the list of traditional correspondences below.

Traditional Erotic Correspondences

Herbs to banish erotic energy: camphor, lettuce, witch hazel, lily, lotus, pepper (color: black)

Herbs to build up erotic energy: apple, cinnamon, daisy, hibiscus, lemongrass, garlic, mint, patchouli, rosemary, vanilla, violet (colors: red, pink, purple)

Other Erotic Accoutrements

The above list is just a smattering of materials that relate to eroticism; it is by no means exhaustive. In fact, the full list runs the gamut from herbs to latex! If you think something is sexy, then it will work as an erotic correspondence for you.

The garter has always been thought of as a particularly sexy article of clothing. Its magical use continues today at weddings when it is thrown and believed to bring marriage to the person who catches it. Today, garters are used to show rank within the coven environment.

The garter can be a powerful tool for inciting lust. To enchant a garter with this task, first soak it in water to which you have added both vanilla extract and hibiscus petals. It is best to do so underneath a Full Moon. Wring it out after twenty-four hours and allow the wind to dry it. Hold it between your palms, clasp your hands in front of your chest, and say something that you consider an affirmation of your undeniable charm. Seal the spell with a kiss, and place the newly enchanted garter upon your leg. This garter is also the perfect place to tie a gris-gris bag if you choose.

One other particularly potent type of magic that is perfectly suited to erotic use is fire and ice. The usage of these two tools is unlimited. You may use them however you wish, just remember to charge the candle and the water before beginning. Many use these items as a tactile sensation by stroking the ice or dribbling the warm wax on the skin.

Happy Erotic Pagans

The Pagan community as a whole has a healthy, positive outlook about erotic adventures and everyday eroticism. It is important to accept this energy as a gift from the divine, and it is correct to celebrate it. It is not necessary to go overboard about sex, but it is correct nonetheless should you feel like embracing your sexuality. Sexual desires are the forebears of life, and all life should be celebrated.

While Mother Nature does enjoy a good joke and is known to send us these vibrations at inopportune times, the energy itself is like a breath of fresh air. It reminds us of the pleasure to be found in life if we one look. Embracing our erotic selves is an easy way for the human body to transcend earthly boundaries and merge with the divine.

Wiccans in the News

by Elizabeth Barrette

Wicca used to be a very obscure religion, hidden from public view and followed only by a few devotees who managed to find it after long searching. Today it is much more open, with thousands of followers worldwide. Some Wiccans "come out of the broom closet" to represent their faith in the public eye. Others prefer to keep their beliefs discreet.

Why the split? Because publicity brings a certain amount of risk. Not everyone shows tolerance and respect to religions different from their own. Wiccans can still lose their jobs, homes, or children because of their faith, although fortunately it happens less often now. As a result, some Wiccans enter the media ring willingly, to serve as spokespeople for their religion, in hopes of promoting tolerance and reducing the number of attacks.

The Problem with Sensationalism

The catch is that newspapers, magazines, radio and television programs, and other media often have divergent goals. While Wiccans want to educate people, the media want to sell advertising space and grab audience attention. Unfortunately, sensationalism sells well. A headline screaming "Watch Out! Witches in West Townsville!" will sell more newspapers than one saying "Townsville Woman Finds Satisfaction in Wicca." This makes it difficult to discourage media producers from running inflammatory material.

Then there is the "formula" issue. Each type of media tends to sensationalize things in a particular pattern. Newspapers and magazines, for instance, like to get articles about "witchcraft" during October to catch the Halloween rush. These articles often are accompanied by stereotypical pictures of green-faced, warty hags. Radio programs often feed on other news sources; once the "buzz" gets going, programmers bring up the topic on a talk show and air the most vociferous callers.

In today's political and social climate, intolerance is growing again. Many people want simple answers and find comfort in "us versus them" scenarios. People feel justified in attacking others different from them or joining attacks made by a mainstream person. Some Wiccans look at the resulting battles and quietly fade away rather than expose themselves and their families to danger. This is costing hard-won ground in public acceptance of alternative religions and lifestyles, though all is not lost.

Legal Considerations

One advantage Wiccans enjoy is the ever-growing archive of legal precedents. Each time Wicca comes into a court case, the ruling

becomes a precedent, and many of the cases resolve in our favor. Some judges have explicitly acknowledged that Wicca is a valid religion, entitled to the same rights and protections as other religions in America. For instance, in Dettmer v. Landon, Judge Williams concluded that "the Church of Wicca is clearly a religion for First Amendment

Some Wiccans have come "out of the broom closet" to represent their religion in the public eye.

purposes." These make excellent references for use in speaking to the media. They also help demonstrate that sensationalistic attacks are harmful and not "all in your head" or "just a joke."

Second, legal cases and policy disputes themselves form a popular subject for media attention. Zoning and tax assessment issues especially tend to come up in local newspapers or radio discussions, often centered around where and how people have the right to worship. Two well-known examples of people defending their freedom of worship involve the Fort Hood Open Circle and the Church of Iron Oak. In such cases, a sympathetic reporter can help educate the public and possibly defuse a stressful situation.

Third, the law offers some protection for Wiccans. We enjoy the right to free speech and protection from defamation. Freedom of expression gives us more of a chance to correct inaccurate statements made by outsiders about our religion. Defamation is an attack on the reputation of another person. According to *The Writer's Legal Guide* by Crawford and Lyons, "For a writer to bring an action for defamation, the defamatory material must have reached the public. Also, the defamatory material must be false, since the truth of the alleged defamatory material will be an absolute defense (except in a minority of states that require, in addition to truthfulness, that the publication be made without malice or for justifiable ends)."

The laws covering libel and slander help discourage the media from publishing material that is legally actionable, and this is especially useful given the temptation to use sensationalism as part of a harassment campaign.

Good and Bad Examples

As Wicca grows, it generates more news. The community becomes more aware of the media and more willing to interact with it instead of hiding. (Some people, alas, still need to remain in the broom closet for their safety; one should only come out if you feel comfortable doing so.)

Politicians spend most of their time in the media spotlight, and sometimes they air their opinions about Paganism. The ABC television program *Good Morning America* once caught George W. Bush, who was Texas governor at the time, saying, "I don't think that Witchcraft is a religion." That statement quickly became known throughout the Pagan community, undermining whatever support he may have had there. It was a mean thing to say, but it provided valuable information, which is news. When something like this comes up, think carefully whether to complain about the negative message or else thank the media for the warning.

Another show, *Mad, Mad House,* featured a Wiccan priestess among its "alts," or people living alternative lifestyles. Fiona Horne had already written extensively about Wicca and was widely known in the community. Some people felt the show would provide good exposure; others felt that it cheapened the religion, or they objected to placing Wicca into the same category with such lifestyles as vampirism. Later *newWitch* magazine ran a feature on Fiona Horne in issue #6, discussing among other things her television appearance and its implications.

The Pagan Pride Day project began in 1998 with just a few small events scattered around America and Canada. Today it is a huge network spanning all fifty states and many foreign countries. Each Pride Day event includes an open ritual, a charitable collection, and notice given to local media. You can read some of the numerous news stories collected on the "News Coverage" page of their the Pagan Pride Day website (www.paganpride.org). This organization generates a fresh wave of positive news every September, so watch for it.

Underlying Principles

The purpose of tracking Wicca in the news is to foster an atmosphere of tolerance and cooperation, thus making the world safer and more pleasant for Pagans and non-Pagans alike. A number of important rules, listed below, apply to all aspects of dealing with the media.

First, you should verify your sources. Make sure you know exactly who said what, and where, and when. If you're following news reports of a given incident, write down the names of people involved, what newspapers or other media cover it, titles of articles and authors' names, air times of radio shows, etc. Don't rely on secondhand reports; check everything yourself.

Know your rights, and stand up for them. Respect other people's rights too, including the media's right to make a decent living.

Never attribute to active malice what can be adequately explained by ignorance. People often say or do things simply because they don't know any better, and they're likely to apologize if you explain the problem.

No matter how obnoxious the other parties involved may get, you need to keep your cool. The more frenzied they become, the more responsible and plausible you will seem in contrast.

Remember that you may be the only Pagan a person has ever met or even heard from. Any member of a minority who deals with the media becomes a kind of ambassador for their culture, so behave accordingly.

Responding to Negative Portrayals

This covers a lot of ground. The media tend to gravitate toward dramatic, scary, and shocking stories of all kinds. Common examples include the media covering a court case in a way that makes the Pagans sound dreadful, publishing letters to the edi-

tor or articles that cast Wicca in a bad light, getting pulled into politicking or interpersonal disputes where Wicca is a bone of contention, revealing someone's religion in such as way as to damage their reputation or livelihood, reprinting obnoxious things that a famous person has said about Paganism, or doing holiday pieces that rehash old stereotypes in ways that can harm contemporary Witches.

What can you do when you encounter an article, radio show, or other newsclip that denigrates your religion? Immediately jot down the details so you won't forget them. Keep copies of printed material and try to get references for spoken examples.

Contact the publisher or producer, cite the offensive material, and politely explain what's wrong with it.

Inquire if they knew beforehand that this material was incorrect, harmful, or violated someone's rights. Give them the benefit of the doubt, and allow them to save face by saying they didn't know. Be sure to ask that they take steps to remedy the misrepresentation.

Ask them to make amends by apologizing for the offense or correcting any inaccurate information in the same venue as the original material appeared. Offer information and resources you have on Wicca that describe the religion's tenets and practices. Mainstream media personnel likely don't have such material at their fingertips, and anything you can do to make their job easier will help endear them to your cause.

If the original portrayal was really horrid and you think it has wider relevance, forward it around the Pagan community. Organizations such as the Lady Liberty League specialize in tracking news relevant to Wicca and other nature religions. This tends to draw a lot of attention to the target media, so if they later change their mind and apologize, make sure you forward word of the retraction to all the places you previously forwarded the offense!

Treat people as professionals. Thank them for their time, and especially for their help if they correct the problem.

Responding to Positive Portrayals

Whenever possible, encourage people for doing good things. The more attention they get, the more likely they will continue and other people may emulate them. Positive coverage can lead to more media attention on the helpful aspects of Wicca. This is a useful resource for times when people are less understanding. Plus, people always enjoy hearing they're doing a good job.

When you see a thoughtful representation of Wicca in the media, here are some things you can do.

Pass the word. Let other Pagans know about it so they can buy a copy.

Save the reference for future use. You can pull it out when you're writing something of your own later, or show it to people who need to know more about Wicca.

Write a letter to the publisher or producer to tell them how much you appreciate their respectful handling of Wicca.

Keep track of which media sources tend to be careful and accurate in their portrayals of minority religions. If you know of relevant news, you can notify them of it first and help them get the scoop on their less-Pagan-friendly competitors.

If you are a Pagan scholar, clergy, leader, or other expert, then you should cultivate a good relationship with whichever of your local media are Pagan-friendly. They may call on you when they need an article or just for a second opinion on Pagan topics.

Taking the News into Your Own Hands

Don't rely on outsiders to tell the world about your religion. Pagans may not proselytize, but we do believe in sharing accurate information with people who want to learn. Too much secrecy makes things seem scary and strange. A more open environment encourages understanding and tolerance.

There are several ways to generate more positive news about Wicca. When you see a negative item about Paganism, express concern to the media and offer to do a counterpoint for them. Many media organizations have a policy of allowing rebuttals.

When you see positive coverage, ask if they'd like more, and include a few suggestions.

Using your list of Pagan-friendly media, keep them posted on events or important accomplishments. The opening of a Pagan-owned business is ideal for local news coverage, for example. Network with large-scale organizations that have a strong media presence, such as the Pagan Pride Day project. Make sure to mention that it's a big project, not just something local.

Even if you don't think of yourself as a writer or a Wiccan activist, you can still make a difference. Anybody can write a letter to the editor. Those are among the easiest things to get published, especially in local media.

Remember that communication is a two-way street. The more people talk about Wicca, the more they learn. Sometimes that leads to gems of literature, other times it just leads to ugly clunkers.

If the media get things wrong, it's okay for Wiccans to speak up and provide a correction, just as Catholics and Jews and other folks do when their religion gets misrepresented. Read thoughtfully, shop wisely in your media selection, and do your best to set a good example.

Live Lightly

by Jennifer Cobb

We are often overwhelmed by the ads that constantly urge us to buy, buy, buy. Daily we are exposed to thousands of pitches for new products of all sorts and varieties, causing sensory overload, anxiety, and, most important, a constant strain on the pocketbook.

In the face of this profusion, our inner voice is drowned out, and we grow more and more overwhelmed by the mad messages of our consumerist culture. Our beliefs and morals and very value systems are be surpassed by messages out of synch with our truest selves. We are titillated and stimulated to buy more than we need or can afford or ever want. We take on more tasks, run more errands, fill our scant time with more activities than we have resources enough to complete. Recent studies show that as a result of the consumer culture, there is actually more incidence of depression, anxiety, unhappiness, and even suicide in Western cultures such as ours.

Simply put, we are heavily burdened with consumerism and its weighty impact on our lives. I, for one, think it's about time to lighten up.

Living Lightly

Living lightly means being aware of what it is we really desire and then freeing up our resources in order to attain just these things. Whether it is joy, creativity, or a natural, excess-free life, we have to choose consciously to free the time and energy for this new focus on light living. We need wisdom to choose wisely when we purchase things, and we need just enough money needed to pursue a light life.

Many people today are consciously choosing to live lightly—to live within their means, and live lightly on the earth—in order to reinvest the excess that would have been swallowed by consumerism into more meaningful things.

Greater Fulfillment

Choosing not to fill our voids with consumerism and its trappings, light livers seek deeper spiritual and emotional fulfillment for sustenance. Whether it is a spiritual practice, meditation, artistic expression, or some form of environmentalism, we let our deepest yearnings and ideals guide our consumer habits, not ads and salespeople.

Whatever the motivation, taking back our decision-making authority, and not simply doing as we are told, is a powerful tool for all aspects of life. When deeply personal choices, morals, and beliefs guide our purchasing and accumulating, how we live then reflects our deeper intentions to the universe. We make the effort to identify what we really need, and invest only in that, and much more falls into place.

Choices, Not Deprivation

Living lightly isn't about depriving ourselves of things, but it is about understanding the impact that consumerist patterns have on our lives, on the lives of other, and on the life of the planet. It is about making choices based on our beliefs, be they environmental, spiritual, or community based.

As Pagans, choosing to live lightly can mean that our Pagan philosophy becomes infused into our everyday practice, and our beliefs then inform our purchasing decisions. Learning to live lightly brings ideals into practice, so we can live fully, magically, and spiritually on the planet, and not as bad parasites. Living lightly is also about lightening the load—clearing clutter, diminishing debt, and taking back time. All of these have implications to our health and well-being.

We need wisdom to choose wisely when we purchase things, and we need just enough money to live lightly.

What We Need to Live Lightly

Learning to discriminate between a need and a want is a powerful step in taking back your awareness of what drives your consumer habits.

Simply put, a need is something that is natural or instinctual; often it is necessary to survival. A want, meanwhile, is something not necessary to survival but that arises from personal preference or a created desire—as stimulated by mainstream marketing or peer influence or some other similar force in our lives.

So the question then is, what do we really need to live? This means, not what advertisers tell us to buy, but what are the basic necessities of life. We can account for many of them: food, clothing, protection from the elements, social connection, loving relationships, regular sleep, and meaningful occupation.

The better the quality of these basic necessities, the better our quality of life usually is.

And yet, advertising tries to sell us lots of stuff that does not fit into this category—shampoos used by runway models, hip sports cars with GPS systems, satellite TVs with 350 stations, empty foods in prime positions at the grocery store, liposuction and plastic surgery, and so much more. Advertisements tell us what will fill the voids in our lives, what will cure our insecurities, what will make up for our lack of social connection or lack of meaningful occupation. Linking false promises to their products, advertisers can make wants look like authentic needs. This in turn leads us to believe that buying such products will satisfy our deeper yearnings. We are sold the illusion that purchasing unnecessary things will fulfill us, enrich our lives, make us happier and better off.

But none of this stuff is really making us happier.

That's the point of living lightly.

What we are urged to spend our time, energy, wisdom, and money on does not satisfy our basic needs, and often these things deplete us of our resources, further emptying us and making us worse off—unhappier and less fulfilled. This, of course, is quite the opposite of the empty promises made by advertisers.

Busier Lives Demand Better Choices

Our lives are busier than ever before, filled with things that consume our resources. The more we buy, the more we have to work to make more money to afford more stuff. It is an endlessly self-perpetuating cycle that results in all of us having less money, less time, less fun, more debt, more worry, more voids to fill, and more unhappiness and stress.

Now, more than ever, North Americans are experiencing debt crisis, with record numbers declaring personal bankruptcy. And its not just financial bankruptcy that is plaguing us. Statistics show that most people don't feel satisfied with the work they do and don't have enough time for the people and activities they enjoy. As a result, many of us rarely feel at peace with ourselves. In the end, consumerism is bankrupting us socially, spiritually, and emotionally.

We have to change our practices of consuming useless goods in order to free up vital resources for making meaningful investment in our quality of life. We have to make better choices if we are to live better.

Live More, Buy Less

Learning to live more and buy less is truly difficult. It means getting rid of the junk in your life—the junk food, the junk that fills our closets, the junky and unfulfilling relationships. We must begin evaluating our life practices and what activities we truly enjoy. We have to ask simple questions of ourselves to determine what is really value in our lives.

> **Learning to live more and buy less is truly difficult; it means getting rid of the junk in your life.**

Examples of such questions include:

Does this (activity, purchase, good) help me be more active, self-reliant, creative, and social?

Does this promote passivity, dependence, and alienation?

Do I really need this?

Will it really bring me joy?

At first such questions feel foreign to our consumerist natures. A lot of emotional baggage is tied up with our consumerism. Whether we eat to stuff our feelings, or buy things to feel better, we often repress the deeper needs that led to the urge to consume. Exposing the deeper needs is truly difficult, but very worthwhile in the end.

So, at first, when you start to evaluate your belongings and practices, don't be surprised if emotions surface—even deep and painful emotions. Letting the emotions arise, rather than keeping them stuffed, will in time bring greater emotional clarity. And, like most good things in life, this energy will grow once it is planted in your spiritual garden.

Emotional clarity will lead to self-evaluation, which will lead to increased clarity and eventually lighter living.

How to Lighten Your Load

Letting go of stuff is tricky at first, but once you get started recycling and giving away your useless belongings, you begin to realize how much energy was stagnating with all the clutter that possessed you. You'll also be able to add up how much it all costs—not just the money to purchase things, but the space to store them, energy to transport them, time and attention to clean and maintain them, and the work required to afford all of these costs.

By thinning your possessions, and then choosing to keep only items you need and enjoy, you'll save a lot of time, space, energy, and money.

The Blue Box

Here's a magical trick you can employ to make this process easier and that you can use as a technique for keeping your load light throughout your life. Try using a magical blue box. Identify materials that are recyclable, then collect, sort, and recycle them. These are any and all items—not just kitchen items, or personal items, or whatever.

In your mind, extend the blue box concept to the living room, collecting books and magazines to pass along to someone else. In the bedroom you could sort through clothes and thin them. What haven't you worn in six months? What is outdated, outsized, or ugly? What clothes don't feel good, look good, or uplift you when you wear them? Help them find a home where they can be loved.

Thinning your possessions starts in one small area of you life. Ask yourself, "Do I love this thing?"

When did I last use this? (If it is longer than six months ago, get rid of it.)

Does this enhance my quality of life or bring me joy?

Can I borrow, share, or rent one of these when I need it?

Sort all the stuff into a few useful piles. The keep pile is for what you cherish, use, and enjoy. These items deserve the investment of your resources. The recycle pile will consist of useful items in good condition that you have no use for. They can be sold,

Letting go of stuff is tricky at first, but once you get started you realize how much energy was stagnating with the clutter.

regifted, or recycled. The garbage pile will consist of stuff that is not in good condition and probably would not be of much use to anyone.

Follow through and do what needs to be done with each pile. Find space for your cherished items in your home, find homes for recycled items elsewhere, and cart the rest to the curb or to the dump.

And don't ever second-guess your purging decisions. Let go of the clutter that possesses you and be free of it forever and always.

Fabulous Living and Spirited Finds

There is nothing wrong with having nice stuff, pretty clothes, pleasing art, and comfortable furniture. Living lightly isn't about denying your needs, so don't misconstrue my message. Instead, living lightly is about linking your consciousness to your consumption and knowing why you buy what you buy so that consumption is a choice you make. The goals is simply to use your purchasing power more wisely.

Living lightly is also about consuming only what is needed and truly appreciated by your household. It is about loving what you need, and needing only what you love.

Treasure Spots

There are lots of treasure hot spots to be explored as you search for pleasing possessions that fall in line with your personal values. For instance, at www.freecycle.org you can join an online community in your geographic area where people post notices of stuff they want to give away and recycle freely. There are also notices about items being sought by others. It is a great way to keep good stuff that you no longer need or want out of the land-fill and find it a loving home.

Don't Forget Garbage Habits

Living lightly extends to our garbage habits too. We can freecycle usable items to the dump, or we can go there to search through other folks cast off items.

Always keep in mind, one person's garbage is another person's treasure. In the city, try dumpster-diving or garbage-rambling through the neighborhood to locate good usable stuff. The end of the month (when renters are most likely to move) and the end of the school year (when students depart from the area) are both great times for seeking out cast-off furniture and household treasures.

Gather with Others

There are many ways you can live lightly in tandem with others of like mind. Form a food-buying club to save money, meet your neighbors, and increase your access to moderately priced good food. A food-buying club requires volunteer involvement in the weighing, packaging, and distributing of food, but it can save the consumer up to half off of retail prices. Even if you are single, a food-buying club can allow you to attain the savings of bulk buying. And you gain a lot of good karma by sharing the goods with like-minded neighbors.

Foraging

Wildcrafting and foraging can also lighten your load. Learn to recognize fruits, vegetables, and herbs that are edible and grow wild in your area. Use a field guide to properly identify the plant, and then keep a little list of where to locate the foods seasonally available to you. If you are ever in doubt, be sure to ask a local expert, as you don't want to make yourself ill. Forage for wild asparagus, strawberries, raspberries, leeks, sorrel, fiddle heads, and dandelion greens. Be sure to give thanks for nature's abundance afterward.

Find Joy in Simplicity

Imagine what you would do if you had more money. Now, ask yourself: How much money have I spent on stuff I didn't truly need or want, or that I could have substituted for with a cheaper item? What if you had that money in your pocket now, what would you do with it?

And, what would you do if you had more time? You don't have to ask the question as a hypothetical—if you choose to live lightly you can let the daydreams roll.

Get Started Living Lightly Today

To take your first steps at living lightly, make a list of all those things you aspire to do but never seem to get around to because you are so busy.

Ask yourself what activities you could limit or cease in order to have more time to yourself. Many of us waste much of our time watching television, overcommitting ourselves, and doing things we don't genuinely enjoy.

Can you envision your life filled only with pleasing and fulfilling activities that you enjoy? Free your time from those poor investments, and reinvest it in yourself and your newly lightly lived life.

In order to have enough time, energy, wisdom, and money to accomplish all that you desire, try to make investments of your resources (of time, money, energy, etc.) that are congruent with your beliefs and lifestyle. Try to be sure that you make of your life what you truly want it to be.

When you consume, always ask yourself if you are being true to your beliefs. Let all of you be present in the decision, so that you don't later regret what you consumed or feel that you spent your scarce resources foolishly.

Choose to live lightly, enjoying greater serenity, clarity, love, and quiet contemplation. Let your deepest desires make themselves clear and guide you to create a rich and joyous life of your own design.

Spread the Good Word

In the end, be sure to spread the good word about living lightly to any and all of your fellow overconsumers. If you feel self-conscious, know that as you simply once did not know there were options to overconsumerism, so likely does the next person simply need to be informed what other options are available in choosing how to live and consume. If the person seems interested, you can tell them more; if not, simply let it rest knowing you did your best.

In this way, person by person, neighborhood by neighborhood, town by town, we can, and will, change habits and so change our consumerist culture for the better.

Living Lightly Resources

Organizations/Websites

Freecycle
www.freecycle.org

Simple Living Network
www.simpleliving.net

Center for a New American Dream
www.newdream.org

Books

Andrews, Cecile. *The Circle of Simplicity: Return to the Good Life.* New York: Harper Collins, 1998.

Burch, March. *Stepping Lightly: Simplicity for People and the Planet.* Gabriola Island, BC: New Society Publishers, 2000.

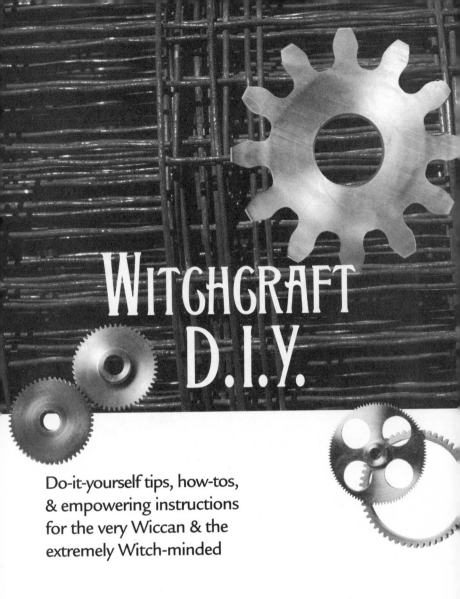

WITCHCRAFT
D.I.Y.

Do-it-yourself tips, how-tos,
& empowering instructions
for the very Wiccan & the
extremely Witch-minded

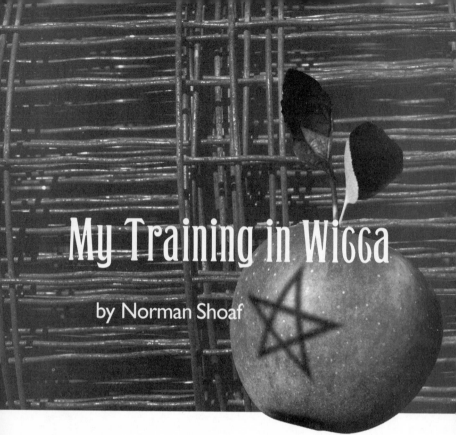

My Training in Wicca

by Norman Shoaf

Note: The following article contains material of a sexually graphic nature that may not be suitable for all audiences. The material is not meant to be sensational or titillating, but instead is one person's personal experience provided as a potential life lesson for any neophytes studying the Wiccan faith.

Study Wicca?

Why not, I thought, when someone asked. It might be a real kick. Some of the nicest people I knew were Wiccans. I've always been fascinated with different religions. And, as I will explain, I had personally experienced the very real power of this ancient, varied, nature-based faith.

What I definitely didn't expect was to become emotionally attached to my teacher, to experience the dark side of magic up close, to find myself bound, gagged, and whipped by a sultry dominatrix, or to have my training ultimately derailed by a shocking turn of events.

Studying Wicca was a kick for me, all right, in more ways than I ever expected.

Into the Circle

I spent most of my life as a conservative Protestant. I got my undergraduate degree from a small Bible college that focused more on facial hair, skirt lengths, and end-time prophecy than on academics. I married a perfectly nice girl I met at that college, and we settled into two decades as pillars in the temple.

Sheltered? Yes. Boring? You bet. Extreme? Yup.

Then my world blew apart, and I went looking for answers.

I was working at a small suburban newspaper in southern California when I broke an outrageous story that eventually went around the world (see "The Incident at Witches Grove" in the 2003 edition of Llewellyn's *Wicca Almanac* for more information).

As I reported, a group of right-wing evangelicals, led by a fire-breathing Protestant preacher who also happened to be a volunteer chaplain with the local sheriff's department, disrupted a Spring Equinox ceremony that a few local Wiccans were celebrating at a private location.

The protesters blared loud Christian rock, invaded a sacred circle, bumped a couple of Wiccan participants, and, when the Wiccans called for help from law enforcement, flashed a business card from the sheriff's department, saying, "No one's coming to help you. You've already lost the war."

When the Wiccans stood their ground, sure enough, the sheriff's department failed to show.

Afterward, the community at large was outraged. I inter-
viewed as many witnesses as I could reach, including many of the

Wiccans whose right to freely express their faith had been trampled. I wrote a series of articles that were picked up by media outlets everywhere, including many Wiccan Internet bulletin boards.

Authorities launched multiple investigations into the hate incident. As a result of my interviews and articles, I was blessed to develop close friendships with many of the folks in our Wiccan community, who—*surprise!*—didn't seem scary at all. They were housewives, students, well-educated engineers, committed twenty-somethings—perfectly decent people that you'd meet next door in any community in middle America.

I spent most of my life as a conservative Protestant and got my undergraduate degree from a small Bible college.

Those Wiccan friends were among the first to respond when a major crisis struck my family and me.

Witchcraft Weighs In

At age forty-five, my wife Pamela, whom I loved dearly and who was also the closest friend I ever had, died suddenly and unexpectedly from a previously undiagnosed ailment, leaving me, our thirteen-year-old daughter, and our three-year-old son alone in shock and grief.

I struggled to find God's purpose in allowing such a tragedy. I longed for comfort and encouragement. The kids, who at such young ages had lost their mother, needed attention.

Several of my Wiccan friends arrived like the cavalry. They provided shoulders for all of us to cry on. They helped with the funeral arrangements. They sat with me, and they took the kids out to McDonald's when I needed a break.

They cast healing circles for us and invited us to take part in very non-Christian energizing supplications to the spirit forces all around us in this world. We did, and we found warmth, safety, sympathy, and trust.

During one of those healing circles with a small number of Wiccans in a private home, we held above our heads a globe of energy that for lack of a better explanation I would describe as a celestial beach ball. We were supposed to lower it slowly and let the ground again absorb it, but at the last second the hostess grabbed whatever force it was and pushed it into my chest, into my aching heart.

I was jazzed more than at any other time I could remember. Newly energized, I barely needed to sleep for the next three weeks, and my dark mood began to lift.

Many of my assumptions from my Protestant background were seriously challenged. This stuff was real—and real good. Did not my own Christian scriptures teach that every good gift comes only from God? I realized there was much more to learn about Wicca, and I wanted to learn it.

At another gathering, the kids and I had tarot cards read for us. The reader, a charming, deep, middle-aged lady who was deadly serious about the activity, told me someone important would come into my life and that the next year would be one of profound learning for me.

A Magical Introduction

A Wiccan lady in her mid-thirties—I'll call her Natasha, though that's not her real name—e-mailed me to express her sympathies on the death of my wife. I recognized her name; she had written to my newspaper to decry the indignities the evangelicals had visited upon the Wiccans. She promised to perform some healing rituals of her own for my children and me. And she said that if I ever needed anyone to talk to or just hang out with, I could give her a call.

During the long, dark, trying months that followed, I did need someone just like that, and I did call. We decided to go out to dinner to talk.

It was one of the biggest turning points of my life.

When I arrived to pick Natasha up at her rural home, I was overwhelmed by her and by her decor.

She was warm, vivacious, and startlingly pretty. In addition to having been a professional model and actress, she had all but completed her certification as a professional counselor. And, she said, she had studied the craft for some fifteen years and was a third-degree Witch.

Her home was stunning. One whole wall of her sitting area was made up of shelves, upon which were stacked jars of herbs, dried plants, spices, incense, and other items. She owned many bejeweled daggers and swords, some of which were lovingly mounted in wall displays. Expertly rendered paintings of mystical fairies and nymphs adorned her walls, for she was a skilled artist. Upon her expensive tables sat enormous glittering crystal balls that must have cost thousands of dollars. A huge fountain commanded one corner of her living room; from it, water flowed into a basin in a soothing, almost hypnotic song.

From the ceiling hung a comical toy bat. When she hit a switch, the bat's beady red eyes lit up and the bat flew around in short circles at the end of its tether. Hanging from the cord on which the bat was suspended from the ceiling was a short whip made of braided leather.

She joked, and we laughed together. We chatted casually while she grabbed her purse and a sweater. She could not have been more charming. I found myself in awe at her open expressions of her faith, and to be honest I was immediately entranced with her.

She was intelligent, kind, funny, and a bit of a tease. As we drove away from her home, she playfully purred, "Are you into B & D? I'm a dominatrix."

So she could read my thoughts, too.

Intrigue and Intimacy

Over the next few months, Natasha and I saw each other for dinner several times. We often talked late into the night. Well, lots of times I talked while she listened sympathetically. She asked insightful questions to help me sort out my thoughts. She offered comfort on those frequent occasions when my grief was unbearable and my tears overflowed.

And we became intimate. She was creative and uninhibited and seemingly could read me like a book. In her attentions I found excitement like I had never experienced, tenderness that cushioned the rough spots over which my life was tumbling, and respite from the demons of dejection and despair.

I genuinely cared for her, and I came to genuinely respect her Wiccan teachings.

Leaving home early and abandoning her family's Roman Catholicism, Natasha began studying Wicca some fifteen years before. She told me she had become a level-one Witch as part of a coven that actually frightened me, as she described it. She said her teacher, a powerful, dark Witch, had appeared to her as she was about to leave for a lesson and reminded her to bring a certain book. At her initiation, she recalled, she had been stripped, bound with rope, blindfolded, beaten, and left in a bathtub full of cold water for several hours.

This didn't sound like any of the Wiccans I knew, but I realized I knew almost nothing.

Worse, Natasha said, when she decided to leave the coven to lead a solitary life, the other Witches had created a puppet, a likeness of her, and imprisoned it in a tub of sticky goo. She said she had been unable to move forward in her life for nearly two years. She tried to sell the house in which she had been living but couldn't get a single offer—this in exploding L.A. county, one of the hottest real-estate markets in the country. When she finally was released, she got as far from the old coven as she could and headed for the rural hideaway she now occupied.

She completed her second and third levels of Witch training, she told me, online.

Strands of Syncretisim

I also learned that Natasha mixed schools of teaching, even religions. She claimed to emphasize Egyptian occultism with Celtic strands of witchcraft, and indeed, in her home were several handsome sculptures of Egyptian gods such as

She could not have been more charming. She was intelligent, funny, and a bit of a tease.

Bast alongside long out-of-print magic texts from England. But she also had, for some time, chanted with Buddhists at a huge Los Angeles temple, and on some evenings I joined her in voicing Nichiren Buddhist chants toward the intricately carved Buddha who sat on her fountain. We lost ourselves in the trances induced by the beautiful, lengthy chants, the seductive aroma of expensive incense, and the majestic, hypnotic tones produced when she struck a large, ornate gong at prescribed intervals.

I knew she also took part in late-night, sky-clad Santerian ceremonies with some leading members of our community, which including ritual inebriation, uninhibited dance revels, and bloodletting, both animal and human. She told me very little about these experiences, although they exerted an irresistible pull on her, and she snickered at what the high and mighty leaders in our right-wing community would think if they knew that some of the area's wealthiest and most influential business people were into voodoo and even Satanic rites.

I didn't leap before I looked. My fascination with the craft and my personal experience of its power grew steadily. At a certain point I made a precipitous commitment, at least to myself.

My Matriculation

I spoke frankly to Natasha about my growing respect for Wicca and about how impressed I had become with her own integrity and commitment. She knew all about my butt-tight background in a legalistic Protestant sect, but I swore of my desire to study Wicca more thoroughly.

She replied that I must ask to become a student. And so I did. I stated that I wanted to study Wicca, and I asked her if she would be my teacher.

In the past, Natasha had taken on a handful of other students. Some arrangements hadn't worked out for one reason or another, but she also spoke proudly of a least a couple students who had devoted themselves to study and advanced dramatically in the craft.

She cautioned me that I should consider seeking training under another Witch, and she named some in our community who would provide a perfectly safe experience. But she openly disdained their practices, describing them as "white Witches" whose paths were commercialized and devoid of real power.

Some of them charged for classes; Natasha found the act of charging for Wiccan knowledge unethical and repugnant. Natasha hinted at the darker, more frightening brand of magic she practiced and candidly warned me it wasn't for everyone.

She did what she called a "reading" on me. She never explained exactly what that entailed or what she learned, but she openly expressed her doubts about whether I could fully, successfully embrace Wicca. Until this point in my life, any religion I had embraced had been mostly "head." If I was to successfully embrace Wicca, I needed to be completely in touch, by contrast, with the "heart," with energies and entities that flourish outside mere rational boundaries.

I didn't want to go halfway with a watered-down class or some pop book I could pick up at Barnes & Noble. I wanted the full ride. I assured Natasha I wanted her as my teacher, and that I would devote myself to serious study. I committed myself to let go and let whatever was to happen, happen.

Thus began a wild course of events that took me beyond the boundaries of anything I had previously experienced and ultimately led to what I now recall, sadly, as a personal life disaster.

Moving Experiences

Natasha began my training by emphasizing to me the importance of the old and the natural. Anxious to begin, I had purchased a fancy portfolio in which to keep class materials and take notes. This she disdained in favor of something simple, handmade perhaps, from wood or natural cloth.

She also was piqued that I instantly went out and purchased books like *Covencraft* by Amber K and *A Witches' Bible* by Janet and Stewart Farrar.

I was not to make such moves unless she directly instructed me to do so. We decided to meet once a week. At my first lesson, she placed an item on her rich coffee table and instructed me to move it using only the power of my mind. She sat back and waited patiently while I summoned every energy I could and concentrated on moving the item. After several frustrating, embarrassing minutes, I admitted failure. She shocked me out of my wits by showing me how to do it, as one might teach a child to drink from a cup.

I have no intention of revealing here how it happened, but believe it or not, I moved the object using only the power of my mind, and I felt that limitations that had long constricted my perceptions were suddenly blowing outward at warp speed, opening innumerable new avenues of possibility to me, utterly freeing me from so many long-held assumptions of "can't," opening for me the whole universe of "can" within the unlimited powers of divine magic.

My very first lesson in Wicca was a totally liberating experience that energized me and lit a hot flame under my desire to absorb, to experience, to feel—as much as I could.

I can sketch in only the briefest strokes how my education unfolded in following weeks: Natasha generously gave me an ornate, intricate, bejeweled dagger from her own personal collection. She showed me how to sanctify it for magical use. She explained the movements of the Moon and the Wiccan calendar of seasons and holidays. We immersed ourselves in the outdoors, with her pointing out for me details I had never noticed. We gathered in circles of our very own, opening unseen doors, calling on the elements, marching clockwise for this, counterclockwise for that. She taught me about the magic of colors, the uses of divination, the awesome powers of meditation and self-abandoning prayer in tandem with the basic force of fire.

Natasha taught me how to create puppets and how to use them. She instructed me in the creation and use of spells. I learned how deadly serious spells are. When some bullies jumped my daughter and son at the playground near my home, she offered me some words and a formula that I carefully followed—and my innocent kids were troubled no more by those personalities; let's just leave it as that.

And she introduced me to the ultimate meaning of the Wiccan pentagram in a blatantly sexual ritual in which we assumed the roles of the goddess Hecate and the god Cernunnos, in which we invited those spirits into our circle and I worshiped at the altar of her breasts, her knees, her feet, and that mysterious, enveloping fount from which all our lives flow.

Oh, yes, magic is real.

All the Way into the Faith

Late one evening, I watched as Natasha carried on a complete conversation while she looked up into the corner of one of her rooms. She claimed to be talking to my late wife, and then she quoted numerous, exact sentences Pam and I had spoken in conversation years before, on a point of my behavior that my late wife had found troublesome. I was dumbfounded. There was no way my teacher could have quoted those conversations so accurately and in such lengthy detail. She had never met Pam, and Natasha and I had never discussed the topic about which Pam apparently was now offering me further advice, through this powerfully psychic Witch.

Natasha and I drove to a remote spot near her home and, in a natural amphitheater shielded by ancient boulders, implored the spirit powers. I devoted myself to prayer, and when I opened my eyes, I found her watching me intently. What she saw, or even whether she was pleased, I do not know. When we returned to town, I effused about the experience and about how happy I had been to share it with her; she responded sternly and suddenly that I was screwing the experience up with misplaced affections toward her.

One night, she emerged from her dressing room wearing only black thigh-length stockings and a luxurious white pullover sweater that fell just below her cute bottom. She told me to strip. She was comfortable in the dominant role, and with all the responsibilities that had fallen on me at home, at work, and in the community, I was relieved to let go and submit to her instructions.

Also, I had already learned that when she wanted something a certain way, I needed to make sure it was that way.

I had been intrigued by the female-centric nature of Wicca; this structure was unlike that of any other religion I knew of, and refreshingly so. All my life I had seen the tragic, sad effect of religions that exalt men while degrading and wasting the value of women, and I had been fascinated by the workings of Wiccan families and male-female relationships in which women obviously took the lead.

One Wiccan teacher told me she regretted having attempted to train a young wife and husband together. I had met this couple and could not have wanted to meet two more pleasant people. The teacher said, with a mischievous grin, that she wished she had taught only the wife and then left it to her to teach her husband so that she "would have something to hold over him."

Natasha produced a ball gag that was made of hard yellow plastic. She told me to open my mouth, and I submissively complied. She shoved the gag in my mouth, said, "Bite down on that," and strapped it around my head. She ordered me to lie down on my back on one of her plush rugs, then quickly roped my wrists together and tied the rope to the leg of one of her heavy tables.

Just like that, I found myself helpless and at my mistress' dubious mercy. I felt a little frightened but intensely excited. She had never hurt me before, but neither was I ever quite sure what her "training" would next involve.

I soon found out.

Natasha produced a leather riding crop and began to whip my buttocks and genitals, playfully and leisurely at first, but increasing in speed and intensity until the rhythm and her ruthlessness created in me a trance of pain and pleasure that I wished would stop and I hoped never would.

Finally, abruptly, she stood over me, lowered herself atop me in a reverse cowboy position and rode me mercilessly. I exploded within seconds. At last she left me there, naked, bound, and gagged on the floor, sore yet tingling, floating in a dreamy sea of rapture and mystified at all the experiences in which Wicca had immersed me. And, yes, I was overcome by a dark, daring, delicious love.

Derailed, and Detached

Now, years later, I harbor no judgments as to the ethics or morals of my experience as a student of Wicca. How can I but embrace the simple, seductive wisdom of the Wiccan Rede I so appreciate: "An' ye harm none, do as thou wilt"?

Natasha inexplicably, uncontrollably broke down in a spell of tears unlike any she had ever experienced.

I know I am larger for the experience, deeper for it, and I look at the world a whole different way, a better way, than before.

But my course of study ended tragically.

Again, I place no labels on what happened shortly after Natasha added the joyous freedom of sexual domination to my education. But one day my training with her suddenly crashed to a halt.

I received a frenetic, slightly frantic call from Natasha. She had been driving in her neighborhood when she came upon a stray dog. She deeply loved animals and shared a special bond with them—she had two beloved dogs of her own—and she had picked the dog up and managed to find its owner.

Natasha told me the dog's owner was overjoyed to have recovered her pet. The lady was an aggressively in-your-face evangelical Christian. She asked Natasha if she would pray with her, and Natasha agreed.

Don't shoot me; I'm only telling you what my soon-to-be-ex-teacher told me. When the woman evoked the name of Jesus Christ, Natasha said she inexplicably and uncontrollably broke down in a spell of tears unlike any she had ever experienced. She told me her heart and mind were flooded with strange feelings and thoughts; she was sure she had literally come into contact with the Christian Savior.

I didn't know what to say, but inside I felt everything slipping away. When I next visited Natasha's home, shortly after her meeting with the Christian lady, I was stunned. Gone was every vestige of the Wiccan identity she had so carefully cultivated for nearly half her life—the wall of ingredients, the crystal balls, the Egyptian and Celtic gods and goddesses, the cauldrons, the black lights, the cutlery, even the toy bat. She had redone every wall and stick of molding with bright white paint. In place of the old items were crosses, angels and cherubs, sugary framed poems, and traditional pictures of Jesus.

She had sold her treasure trove of Wiccan accoutrements, Natasha told me, and donated the money to the church to which her new friend belonged. And what she hadn't sold, she had either given away or just trashed.

Our classes were over, of course, she said. If I wished to continue to study Wicca, she told me, that was fine with her, but it would have to be with someone else. Perhaps one of the "white Witches" would take me on as a student. We could stay friends, but she intended to pursue her new relationship with Christ with the same fervor she had devoted to her now-discarded Wiccan faith.

She had saved one final gift for me: As I left her house, she handed me the braided whip that had hung with the bat. She no longer wanted it in her home.

In a mere span of days, though, even her suggestion of "friendship" changed. In this short time, she realized that I had Satan in me. She could see the devil in my eyes, she said. I had evil inside me, and she urged me to go get "delivered," just as she had been by her new friend and the members and pastor of the hardcore, neo-Pentecostal Jesus cult to which she had so suddenly committed her life and energies.

They had prayed over her. They had cast out the spirits in her. She had vomited. She had become dizzy and lost consciousness. She had awakened in a different room, and a pentagram had mysteriously appeared on her stomach.

She urged me to follow the same course.

I had no intention of doing any such thing. Instead I felt bewildered, betrayed, and ultimately cast adrift in an ocean of confusion. I suppose I had been expelled from the loosely organized

University of Wicca—or rather, perhaps, the school had somehow tragically burned down.

Will you understand if I tell you it hurt too much at the time to try to continue my Wiccan journey?

An' Harm None

I respect everyone's right to believe and practice as they see fit. But I can't see how I would ever again entrust eternal currency to the hands of any changeable (read: potentially unstable) mortal. I suppose I'm left with simply trusting the benevolent intelligence of our awesome universe to carry me where I'm supposed to go. Maybe that's the bottom line of all legitimate faiths—with the added directive, which every major religion embraces, to love our neighbor as ourselves.

Still, I often think about the sublime, satisfying pursuit of the ancient, natural wisdom and insights of Wicca under a caring, knowledgeable, legitimate, and responsible Witch. And if she was possessed of a naturally dominant streak, a playfully mischievous personality, and she knew how to tie a decent knot, well, so much the better, right?

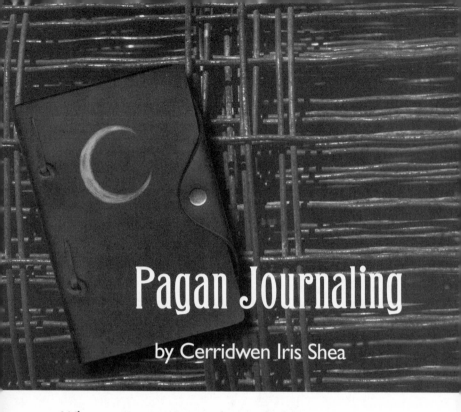

Pagan Journaling

by Cerridwen Iris Shea

What separates Pagan journals from the average, ordinary "Dear Diary" or those online blogs that seem to be everywhere now? In addition to the variety of journal options—grimoires, mirror books, books of shadows—what sets Pagan journaling apart?

The answer: content.

Pagan journaling differs from even the most religious journals in the content. It doesn't matter if you choose to share your feelings publicly on an open blog, or to privately scribble in a notebook, because Pagans deal with simultaneous planes of existence. Pagan journals are different from typical journals. There is no "I did *blankety-blank* today, and I felt *humbledy-dum* doing it. *Yadda yadda yadda.*"

Don't get me wrong—there's nothing wrong with a simple chronicle. But being a Pagan isn't linear, and neither is Pagan journaling.

The Many Forms of Pagan Journals

The grimoire, the mirror book, and the Book of Shadows all have specific tasks in a Pagan's life. And so does a journal. But the Pagan journal is more free flowing. It can encompass some or all of the other three kinds of books, but takes things even further.

A Pagan journal chronicles, analyzes, and offers a place for you to write in a stream-of-consciousness style. It also offers a place to experiment with ideas and life choices.

I don't remember where I first heard of it, but a few years ago, I came across something called an "alternate journal." This was a fictional journal kept by someone, somewhere, about the life he wished he was leading. In other words, it was a Walter Mitty–esque fantasy journal. I don't remember the actual details, but the idea itself intrigued me.

Pagans work with affirmations all the time. Many books talk about reprogramming one's subconscious in order to create and recreate one's reality.

Why not do that with a journal? Why not take the meditation and positive thinking techniques we try to put into practice and write our own reality in our journal? Why not magically write ourselves into our best lives?

Active Magic through Journaling

According to Marta Hiatt in her book *Mind Magic,* the subconscious mind works in the present. This means that in a magical journal your affirmations must be worded in the present, rather than in the future. In your Pagan journal you must write toward

the life you crave in the future as though it exists right now, in the present.

For instance, if you want a house, use a few pages of your journal to write about finding the house— what it feels like, what the house looks like, what the neighbors are

In your Pagan journal you must write toward the life you crave in the future as though it exists in the present.

like, and so on. Write about painting the house, moving into the house, filling it with furniture, hanging pictures on the wall, and becoming comfortable there.

In this practice, you're creating positive energy to pull you and the house together like magnets. Does it mean that you will find the exact house you envision? Will all be identical to your entries? No. But it does mean you are putting the energy into motion, and you're telling your subconscious this is a reality.

In Pagan journaling, you are not doing a binding magic to keep yourself from finding the best house for you simply because you deal with specifics in the journal. (You might choose to enhance this magic through an encompassing ritual separate from the journal work to draw the best possible dwelling to you.) But by journaling your intention you are setting magical energy in motion.

Journaling Exercises

For exercises of the sort listed above, I suggest keeping a separate journal book from your normal Pagan journal. Give this new book a title that energizes you, as this is the book where you create your positive, affirmed, new existence.

Having two journal books doesn't mean when you go back to your normal daily journal about what actually happens in your life that your entries cancel each other out. Remember, when you meditate or say affirmations, you spend sacred time in sacred space to do the work, and then you release it. "Affirmative

Journaling," as I call it, is similar to this basic divide between the divine and mundane.

Make sure that your wish journal is beautiful and that you are mindful of the time and space in which you write. Make it a ritualized event. Consider the opening of the book the start of a ritual. Closing it is the end. And when you close it, you release it, and go about your day.

The Natural Impulse in Pagan Journals

I've noticed another difference between "regular" journals and my Pagan journal and those of my Pagan friends: our journals tend to run more along the lines of naturalists' journals, even if we're urban. We notate the weather, Moon phases, retrogrades, birds we see, trees, flowers, and so on. Because the natural world has a strong impact on our Pagan lives, it turns up more frequently and in more detail in our writing.

That tendency aids us in mindful living and attention to detail. For instance, on the next sunny day, take your journal out to a favorite spot in the park or your favorite café. Write about where you are at that moment.

What do we say after casting a circle? ("Be here now.") Well, this is a perfect time to be here now—and write about it!

Pagan journals also deal with the otherworld. It's a place to work on intuitive and clairvoyant skills. It's a place in which to explore other realms and dimensions. You can experiment with automatic writing in the safety of your journal. It's a perfect place to work on and learn about your dreams or the imagery that comes up in meditation.

So many people deal with merely one world—we deal with many! We're so lucky! And our Pagan journals can help us keep a more constant contact with the worlds.

Journaling for Fun and Profit

Journaling is a way to sort out our possibilities, our options, our goals, and our dreams. It's a way to explore relationships with fairies and devas and angels and spirit guides and any other entity with which you are in communication. It's a perfect way to sort out what works in our lives and what still needs to be changed.

In our journals we can write our way into those changes, magically transforming our lives.

The only rule of journaling is to date your entry. That way, when you go back, you can place the entry in the context of what was going on around you at the time. Although at the time you write you believe you'll remember everything about the moment, the fact is you won't. Do yourself a favor for later and date the entry.

> No matter your path, journaling is a useful tool for growth, exploration, analysis, and spurring positive change.

I find weather, Moon phases, and place important to note, too, because these affect my emotions and may help provide clues to what I was feeling when I wrote, but this is a personal choice. You may choose to note completely different details in your journal entries—whatever you think may be useful later or fun to read is perfectly acceptable.

The Possibilities Are Endless

No matter what your path, journaling is a useful tool for growth, exploration, and analysis. Keeping a journal—especially a magical Pagan journal—is a way to provoke positive change.

In your journal, you can detail all the joys and sorrows of your life. You can write yourself through pain and into beauty. For Pagans, journaling is a way of expanding our multidimensional lives and also a way to set them down and sort them out. It's a way to capture memories and take the first steps in manifesting our dreams.

The possibilities for journals are as infinite as the universe.

Books of Interest

Baldwin, Christina. *Life's Companion: Journal Writing As a Spiritual Quest*. New York: Bantam, 1990.
Many of her ideas support Pagan views, and she offers techniques for making the journal an entity in one's daily life rather than a chore.

Johnson, Alexandra. *The Hidden Writer: Diaries and the Creative Life*. New York: Anchor Books, 1998.
The author analyzes how journals affected the lives of women such as Margery Fleming, Virginia Woolf, May Sarton, Alice James, and Anaïs Nin.

Mallon, Thomas. *A Book of One's Own: People and Their Diaries*. St. Paul, Minn.: Ruminator Books, 1995.
A collection of journals and diaries through the ages.

Sarton, May. *Journal of a Solitude*. New York: W.W. Norton & Co., 1992.
Poet and writer May Sarton is most famous for her published journals, and this is the one that shot her to fame. Written over the course of just over a year, when she bought her house and started a new life alone, she talks about the ups and downs of a creative life.

Free Blog Hosts

For those who are adventurous enough to want to put their journals online:

http://www.blogspot.com

http://www.livejournal.com

http://www.blog-city.com

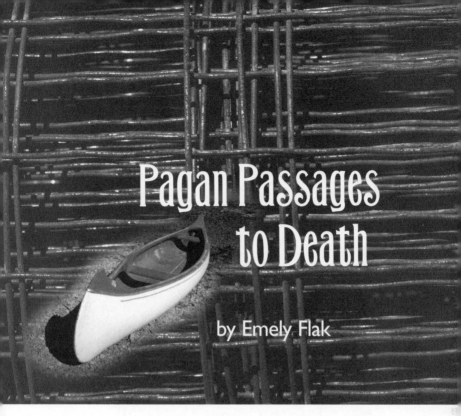

Pagan Passages to Death

by Emely Flak

There's a popular expression that says: "The only certainty in life is death and taxes." We all know that death, at some point in time, is inevitable. What varies, however, is the way we honor this rite of passage, as there are endless possibilities. Even the words used to describe the last rite differ—as we can hear it called a funeral, a memorial service, a tribute, or a celebration of a life.

Evidence in ancient burial sites suggests that a final rite has been carried out for the deceased for tens of thousands of years. Over time, as different cultures and

religions developed their interpretation of the divine, they each also carved out their philosophies about what happens after we die. Today, the way in which the last rite, or funeral, is performed depends on the cultural and spiritual traditions and the wishes of the deceased and the deceased's family.

Death Comes to Us All

Despite the inevitability of death, dying and grief remain poorly understood and rarely discussed topics. Very few of us talk openly about death or feel at ease comforting a dying friend or relative. When a member of our family dies, the next-of-kin arranges the funeral or memorial service. Often it is not something that we plan in advance. In fact, the ceremony for the last rite is arranged relatively quickly at a time when we are struggling mightily to manage our feelings of grief.

Despite the mystery that surrounds death and dying, the ways in which we honor the deceased in Western society is slowly changing. For instance, it was once considered taboo to bring a child to a funeral service. It is now regarded as an important way to help children say goodbye and accept loss as part of the life cycle.

For most people, the funeral is increasingly becoming a tribute and celebration of life rather than a perfunctory or somber service that lacks a personal touch. The final tribute is now regarded as an occasion to celebrate the life of the person who has passed away, as well as a time to mourn them.

Considering the Inevitable

Although the cultural approach to funerals is changing, how many of us consider how we want our own final rite to take place? Or what do we arrange when a Pagan friend or loved one has passed away?

At first, one would think a Pagan funeral should be straightforward to organize. We generally follow a belief system based on the wheel of the year that represents birth, death, and rebirth. As a result, most of us are familiar with common Pagan rituals, symbols and elements. Surely, a last rite would be based on these principles.

> Despite the inevitability of death, dying and grief remain poorly understood and rarely discussed topics.

But despite our Pagan path, the way in which we say goodbye to our loved ones and the way we view death is not always the same.

We want to create and perform a rite that truly honors them in an uplifting way, as a tribute to their life and shared memories while respecting their individual preferences. Yet with so many variations in Pagan practice and beliefs about death, it is almost inevitable that there is a great confusion in the Pagan world about what constitutes proper Pagan rituals for death.

The First Generation Pagan

Unless our Pagan friend has clearly defined with next-of-kin his or her wishes for the final rite, we may face family members with little empathy for or knowledge of Pagan beliefs. The next-of-kin will arrange a service that represents, in their view, the life and philosophies of the deceased. As a result, the funeral service is likely to take place in a church.

For example, a family with strong Christian traditions may show little tolerance for alternative spirituality or might have never even known that the deceased was a practicing Pagan. Either way, during this sensitive time, even if once close to the deceased and more aware of his or her beliefs and spiritual values, we are obliged to respect the family's decisions.

Regardless of our religious background, when a loved one dies, the grief unites the family and friends mourning the loss. If the family opposes a Pagan service, you can conduct a memorial service with appropriate themes and references at a separate time for your first-generation Pagan friend.

Grief

Despite our religious beliefs, the death of someone close to us affects us all, but not always in the same way. Each person deals with grief differently.

Sadly, it's when someone knows he or she will die or when he or she is experiencing grief over a lost loved one, that the person feels most isolated and needs human contact the most. The work of Elisabeth Kübler-Ross, in her book *On Death and Dying*, helped change the view of death and grief. In her study and published material, she has identified five stages of dying that are felt by those who know they are dying and by the ones grieving. They are denial and isolation, anger, bargaining, depression, and acceptance.

Denial and Isolation
In the denial and isolation stage, the person talks about the future and avoids discussion on the issue of death. In this stage, there is much room for fantasy and unrealistic promises and thinking that ignore the reality of death.

Anger
The second stage of anger typically sees the person facing the reality with feelings of anger that can result in losing faith in reli-

gious beliefs. The person can also begin casting accusations at family and friends, charging them with a lack of caring and a loss of love for the dying person.

Bargaining
When experiencing the bargaining phase, the person has expressed anger and tries to make a "pact" or "promise" with a higher, divine force to negotiate and extended life. This will manifest in a promises such as "If I live a bit longer I promise to look after my diet and body better and to do only good in the world," or "If I resolve all my issues with my parents, then I will deserve better than this." This phase is not relevant to grieving family and friends.

Depression
In the fourth stage, depression is felt. Here, the dying person understands that death is inevitable and realizes the reality of the loss. The loss can be felt at varying levels. For example, loss of a partner can result in the end of financial security, as well as the end of emotional security and intimacy. Special events that intervene—such as birthdays and anniversaries—can also trigger this depression.

Acceptance
In the final stage, acceptance, the person who is dying will lose interest in worldly events and may wish to be left alone. At this stage, family and friends (following a death) will begin to heal.

The Impact of the Five Stages
In fact, nowadays very few discussions about grief and dying take place without reference to Kübler-Ross. In her work, Kübler-Ross also identified that because death is a universal fear, medical staff are poorly trained and uncomfortable with the notion and realities of death and dying. In turn, the people dying or grieving can end up feeling isolated and alone in their emotions.

Understanding these five stages can actually help us all to identify our own grief and in the end assists us in better sympathize with others dealing with such loss. The more we know about these stages and the process of dying, the better equipped we are all to deal with it.

Coping

We feel grief when we experience the transition to a life without our loved one. Here are some practical ways to cope with this grief and loss.

First, talk to family and friends. After a tribute or funeral service, mourners often disband and manage their loss alone. If you feel isolated, you may need to discuss your feelings with others. It is also important to keep up social activities to minimize feelings of isolation.

Second, read books about the subject. Learning about the grieving process helps you understand the cycles and gain an insight into other people's experiences and how they coped with such loss.

Third, nurture yourself. Maintain your routine of self-care with a sensible diet, ample, exercise, and keeping up your personal appearance.

Fourth, join a support group or seek counselling. If you are not comfortable talking to family and friends, look for a group or counselor. A person removed from the situation can offer a different level of support.

Finally, allow yourself to grieve through the stages identified by Kübler-Ross. Acknowledge that you will experience emotional swings; at times you will want to be alone and at other times you will crave the company of others. Be willing to go with the emotional tides, and recognize if they devolve into something negative and beyond your control you may need to seek professional help and counselling.

The Tribute

Let's assume that you will conduct a Pagan funeral service or tribute for a lost loved one. Even if you have attended a Pagan last rite before, you will need to plan it to ensure that it is a special, customized farewell for your friend. Although there is no prescribed doctrine in Paganism or Wicca on death and the afterlife, it is generally accepted that most of us believe in reincarnation and the Summerland.

The Summerland, a place where our soul rests as it contemplates our life lessons, is consistent with the Wiccan Rede and the concept of living our lives with full responsibility for our actions. There might be variations in the focus of the last rite depending on specific Pagan traditions or mythology. For example, if your practices were aligned to Norse traditions, you would refer to the Summerland as Valhalla.

Preparation

The preparation is as important as the delivery. Keep in mind that the preparation time for a final rite is usually very short. It is expected that the funeral take place within a few days of the passing. Use this checklist to help you plan a tribute.

Location
Indoors, outdoors, public venue or a private home? As a nature-based spiritual path, one might expect a Pagan funeral to take place outdoors, but there may be times, especially in cold climates, when this is not feasible.

Eulogy
A eulogy is the speech that praises and describes the deceased,

highlighting key events and milestones in his or her life. Consider carefully: Who will read the eulogy? Will you engage the services of a civil celebrant? What will the eulogy mention? Whom should you go to for information?

Reflection Time

In almost every funeral there is a short period during which family and friends reflect on their memories of the deceased during silence or with music playing in the background. Think about the music that will be played; often this is the dead person's favorite music. Decide if people will come forward during this time to make offerings to the coffin. What will these offerings be? Flowers? Incense? Small gifts?

Special Readings, Stories, Songs, and Poetry

Sharing funny stories adds balance to what can be a somber occasion and turns it into a meaningful tribute. Always take take care that the humor not offend family members or close friends.

Altar Preparation

As an object of focus, what will you place on the altar? What color or colors will you choose for the altar cloth, incense, flowers, and candles? White is usually associated with death and rebirth. Will you add photos, favorite possessions of the deceased, or items hand-crafted by him or her?

The Farewell

Will the deceased's body be at the service? Will it be a burial or cremation? How will you farewell or "commit" the body? Will you play a final piece of music, sing or read a piece of poetry?

Special Rituals

There are many special additional rituals that can make the ceremony that much more unique and special. For instance, what will you need for additional rituals, such as sharing of bread and wine? Will there be an offering? You may wish to provide a flower for each person, or offer apple pieces to symbolize renewal and rebirth. Do you want music or drums?

If you know someone who is talented with drums, this effectively and quickly creates a sense of sacred space. If you cannot use drums, music influences the atmosphere. At some Pagan funerals, the priest or priestess rings a bell to bless the person as they cross over to the Summerland.

Circle Casting
Casting circle enhances the ceremonial atmosphere, but this may be inappropriate depending on the location of the service and level of grief felt by the mourners.

Check Out State Legislation
It is important to consider state law before planning any death ceremony. Will it prevent you from carrying out rituals such as scattering ashes or using public parks? Some laws may require that a registered celebrant carry out the final rite.

As you can see, there are many possibilities to consider.

Performing the Last Rite
To help you structure your Pagan farewell, include these three elements in your final rite: the opening, the celebration of life, and the closing.

Opening
Set the scene with drumming or music. Announce the purpose of the gathering and create a sacred space; cast circle if you wish. Introduce yourself and your relationship to the deceased. Remind everyone to switch off cell phones.

Celebration of Life
Deliver the eulogy and invite others who wish to speak, sing, or read poetry to honor the deceased. Use this time for any special rituals and reflection time.

Closing
When the deceased's body is at the final rite, it concludes with the "committal." The committal is the time when body is committed either to the element of earth (burial), to the element of

fire (cremation), or less frequently to the element of water (sea burial). You might wish to bury or cremate your loved one with favorite ritual tools, a talisman, or tarot cards.

If the deceased's body is not at the service, you can perform the farewell with words, verse, or song as they commence on their next journey. A popular way to say goodbye is to sing "We all come from the Goddess," as each person offers a flower from the altar to the casket. Close the circle or say words to declare the end of the ritual. Thank everyone for participating in the farewell. After the official ritual, set aside time for an informal gathering, either at a public venue or at a private home, to talk about your loved one and share some food and drink.

What We Can Do in Advance

We face a difficult situation when a loved one has a terminal illness and knows he or she will soon die. Even with knowledge about the five stages of dying, this is a time that challenges us as we are forced to face our own mortality. We confront that awkward issue that Western society has poorly prepared us to discuss.

Death and dying are topics that remain largely taboo and feared by our culture. As a result, we rarely discuss the issues. If your Pagan group meets regularly for discussions, arrange a session to talk about this subject. This discussion will help you gain an insight into how your Pagan friends view death and how they wish to be farewelled.

Even though it's not likely everyone will agree, it will help you explore your own thoughts more deeply. Talking openly in advance helps all of us deal with our own grief, and it helps others who need our support when they have experienced the loss of a loved one.

It's generally accepted that Pagans celebrate the wheel of the year that represents birth, death, and rebirth. However, the way we perceive death and how we manage grief is a deeply personal experience. There is really no right or wrong way to carry out a final rite of passing for a Pagan friend or family member. Some ceremonies are sad, some are filled with happy memories, and some will contain a mixture of emotions depending on the circumstances.

If you feel that your Pagan loved one has not been farewelled in a Pagan way, due to family or next-of-kin preferences, don't feel short changed. In a separate ritual, acknowledge the deceased and say goodbye using Pagan themes. Creating and conducting a last rite is a loving act that requires thought and preparation, unites a group, and helps all deal with taboo loss and grief.

A Pagan Farewell

My loved ones, my circle,
Cry not for me.
I am resting in the Summerland
You will see.

This is our heaven,
Our place of rest,
To contemplate the life lessons
My soul has learned the best.

Here I can stay
And watch over you,
And I can continue my journey
Of rebirth too.

I have simply shed a body
That no longer worked for me,
But my soul and spirit are forever.
I am with you, you are with me.

Death, birth, and rebirth
Are cycles not to fear.
In the arms of the Goddess
I am still to you so near.

My loved ones, my circle,
Do not cry for me.
I am not far in the Summerland,
In time you will see.

Recommended Reading

Kübler-Ross, Elisabeth. *On Death and Dying*. London: Tavistock Publications, 1969.

Sweep Me Away!

Tips & suggestions
for Wiccans who wander
through the wide &
wondrous world

Thumbprint Travel

by Cerridwen Iris Shea

I have to give credit where credit is due: I did not coin the term "thumbprint travel." My first exposure to it was in one of Susan Allen Toth's lovely books on traveling in Britain. I'm not sure if the volume was *England as You Like It*, *England for All Seasons*, or *My Love Affair with England*. But no matter, in one of these volumes she talks about her "thumbprint theory of travel."

By this she means that whenever she travels she picks a single place to stay and does not venture from that spot farther than a radius that can be covered by her thumb on a map. Depending on the size of

one's map, that area can be quite large, or quite small. I tried it once on a map of the world and three small countries fit into my thumbprint. On a street map of a town, it could limit you to the local cemetery.

Under My Thumb

My modification of her thumbprint travel notion is to have a central location in mind for a trip, and to take small, relaxing day trips during the vacation. In this way I can avoid spending all my time on the road and returning from my trip even more exhausted than I left. By having a temporary but stable home base, venturing forward from there, and then returning for relaxing evenings, I stay calm and unstressed even as I learn in depth about the area I am visiting. Instead of merely scratching the surface, racing around, and winding up exhausted, I connect with the place and keep my sanity.

Connection with place is an important part of my practice and my path.

This also means taking the time to research my location and choose a home base that will be comfortable. I check the Internet. I look in bookstores and the library for travel guides and essay books about the place in which I'm interested. I check sites such as Journeywoman.com for travel tips. I talk to people. I contact the chamber of commerce or the tourist board.

I don't need the height of luxury when I travel. What I do need is a clean, simple, safe place, preferably with a kitchen. When traveling in the U.K., I rent from the National Trust. For less than the price of a hotel room, you can rent an entire property, usually with a garden. Part of your rental fee goes to the upkeep of the property you've rented. The rest goes to buy up other properties to prevent them from being paved over or turned into strip malls.

So how does thumbprint travel fit in with Pagan values? It works on several levels. First of all, in a situation such as renting from the National Trust, you help preserve and maintain the natural environment. A row of cottages with gardens and trellises of climbing roses versus a strip mall: Is that really a difficult decision? Not for Pagans.

Thumbprint travel also gives you a sense of place. You connect with local devas. You can perform rituals in the garden. Most of the places I've rented are private enough for you to be your Pagan self. You buy produce from the local farmers, supporting the local economy. You prepare healthy food instead of eating every meal out—yet you also have the option of going out to eat and supporting the local economy by patronizing its restaurants. You interact with the commu-

I stay calm and unstressed even as I learn in depth about the area I am visiting.

nity instead of imposing on it. You learn the history and mystery of place. In addition to renewing your spirit, you in turn, renew the place you visit. It's far more interactive than passing through and staying in a motel.

When you create a home base instead of staying in constant motion, you also create sacred space. Instead of racing around, you live mindfully in the space. Everything is a discovery—from finding where the coffeepot is kept, to learning what that bird is landing on the feeder in the yard, to eating your meals in the glassed-in conservatory as you watch the Sun set over the land. There's a sense of being completely in the moment, listening to the past, celebrating the present, and honoring the future.

Some Magical Thumbprint Tips

When you enter your rented sacred space, take the time to read over the instructions left for you. Don't wait until something goes wrong. Be prepared in advance. Even if the space is clean, clean it yourself. Smudge it, if you can. Sweep. Talk to the house and the garden. Introduce yourself. Light a candle, connect with the place—the guardians, the devas, whoever looks after the property. Make a libation.

Unpack on your first night. Make the space yours. I like to go grocery shopping on the way to the place so I can fill the cupboards. I also buy a bottle of wine and fresh flowers on my way there. Both of those objects help me feel connected and at home. I like to create a spontaneous "Welcome" ritual in order to connect with the place.

Treat the property gently and with reverence. Enjoy the differences between it and your normal environment. By carefully

THUMBPRINT THEORY OF TRAVEL

choosing where you stay, you spend more time on site and less time running around. Why dash to every tourist trap when you have a lovely, tranquil garden waiting for you at your temporary home?

If something goes wrong, look at it as an adventure, rather than a tragedy. Stay in communication with the caretaker. Once, in Cornwall, I had to call the caretaker to come and help me change a light bulb. It had an odd locking device on it I'd never encountered before, so I couldn't make the change myself. Was it frustrating to stand there in the fading light, waiting for someone to drive forty minutes to help me? Yes. But it was also lovely to watch the colors change across the yard—the rising blues, grays, and reds of the fading light touching the yellow blossoms, the green grass, and the pockmarked tree bark. And the caretaker arrived before I needed to use the flashlight, so it was fine!

It's exciting to venture out and explore your region. And it's satisfying to come "home" at night, to be able to sit in the yard with a cup of tea or a glass of wine and eat in the glassed-in conservatory, watching the sunset over the meadow, sitting in the old brocade wing-backed chair with your feet on the needlepoint stool, reading a book a former tenant left behind. Also, as you make friends in the region and accept invitations, you can issue your own. You can be as involved or as anonymous as you choose.

> **It's satisfying to come home at night to sit in the yard with a glass of wine, watching the sunset over the meadow.**

Thumbprint Day Trips

A wonderful aspect of taking a day trip is that you're not too tired from the travel to actually enjoy the destination. You visit places close to your home base rather than just waving at them as you pass by. On a dreary day with sputtering rain, instead of driving to the garden six hours away, go to the local museum in the little house beside the village church. Have tea and eavesdrop on the local gossip. You'll be glad you did. You'll stop and visit places you might have missed otherwise, because you were once so fixated on getting "there." Just wait till you see what happens when you concentrate on "here."

Since I'm addicted to libraries, I usually make sure I spend time in the local branch, learning about history and writing about it in my journal (which later leads to articles and fiction). As long as you treat the books with reverence, local librarians are happy to visit with you. Often, they will share fascinating tidbits of information you couldn't find anywhere else.

Decide how much time you're willing to spend on the road each day, and plan accordingly. Most rental units have a folder of information with local attractions. Or else you can stop at the visitor information center, the grocery store, or, best of all, at the local pub. Everyone has a particular favorite place or some attraction that might not make it into the tourist guides, but of which locals are proud. Find them. You'll stack up memories that will keep you smiling for years to come.

Gathering the Riches of Local Places

With thumbprint travel you'll find there's no such thing as "nothing to do." You'll have no reason to be bored unless you're a boring individual. And, as you know, Pagans aren't boring.

One of the joys of being a Pagan in this life is that everything in the natural world is interesting to you. And now, thanks to these simple travel concepts, you get the chance to enjoy it while you're on vacation.

Closing the Thumbprint Circle

When it's time to leave, be certain to do a ritual of thanks. Again, give a libation. Clean the place thoroughly, leaving it even better off then you found it. (This is not only basic courtesy, but it follows basic Pagan ideals.)

If you've moved furniture because it felt better to you, return it to its original placement. Many properties have a guest book—take the time to write up a memorable entry. While you're there, take the time to read other people's entries. Often they will mention a place visited or a favorite restaurant that you will enjoy, which perhaps you can stop at on your way out of the region.

Above all else, seek to feel a connection to past visitors and to create a reason for future visitors to connect to you. You never know where such energies will lead.

Nowadays, we're forced to rush so often in our daily lives. We work too long hours and seldom slow down to take care of ourselves. Even our daily leisure activities—watching TV, surfing the Internet, and so on—generally take away from our ability to relax and turn off our overloaded brains.

In a time when travel, especially by air, has gotten more and more frustrating and stressful—as most corporations put their head executives' profits ahead of any pretense of customer service, and terrorism is in the back of all of our minds—you will do yourself a great favor by learning how to take vacations.

By traveling mindfully and covering small areas of territory thoroughly and with joy, you will return with a refreshed spirit and perhaps even some new muses.

Urban Nature Spirits

by Diana Rajchel

Heinrich Cornelius Agrippa taught this essential lesson about the nature of the four elements to budding Renaissance-era occultists:

"There are four Elements, and originall grounds of all corporeal things, Fire, Earth, Water, Aire, of which all elementated inferiour bodies are compounded; not by way of heaping them up together, but by transmutation, and union; and when they are destroyed, they are resolved into Elements. For there is none of the sensible Elements that is pure, but they are more or less mixed, and apt to be changed one into the other."

Agrippa also wrote that all bodies of mass in this plane—the elemental plane—consist of compounds of multiple elements. So that which we perceive as fire really consists of fire, air, and earth: the flame as fire, the fuel from earth, and air for the necessary combustion to result in "fire." A pebble on the ground classified as earth is really earth because water gave it form, air determined its mass, and fire reshaped it into the pebble I am now kicking absently over the street.

All elements require the other elements to stay present.

This mixing of elements occurs on all levels. That is, something is always part of everything else.

Thus, nature spirits do not distinguish their address based on zip code, trees, or annexation. The part belongs to the whole, and all elements require other elements to stay present, whether in the form of simple water bonding or in the complex synthetic-organic dance of urban petroleum and plastic.

The Compounds of Nature

Even twenty floors above the ground, earth, air, fire, and water exist in compounds. Consequently, so do the elemental spirits that live within the elements in their varying forms. A dryad may live on as your wooden cupboard. A light bulb could house a (very frustrated) salamander. The garbage dumpster probably has gnomes. The spirits live all around you, adapting, and adopting just like any other evolving species.

It's a common assumption that the miles of concrete at the center of a city divorce its residents from nature. This isn't true. Nature rules over all, and no tall building or parking lot can deny the power of nature—say, in the form of a tornado or an earthquake. No mass transit can stop a rainy day.

Only through determination and severe agoraphobia can a city resident avoid the outdoors and what it brings. And sometimes even the most determined voluntary shut-in is met by a

leaky roof, a cold day, or some other aspect of nature tapping at the door with a friendly reminder that nature really makes the rules. The longing for "nature" expressed by fans of thorough and agrarian-based Paganism comes from a desire for a cleaner, simpler lifestyle. But, contrary to comments I've heard, a city is in no way separate from nature. In fact, the city is just as much under the dominion of natural cycles and weather.

No matter how old, a city is no more than a mere blip on the face of geological history.

Agrippa's lesson on the elemental plane can extend to the full experience of this reality. Everything viewed as matter, as touchable, as present, comes from a composite of elements.

Everything that is, traces back to a single source. Pure elements can't exist safely in this plane, and their exposure causes a near immediate corruption, wherein the particles join up with other particles until the pure element forms a composite.

Manifestation of the Modern Spirit

In nature, these composites manifest as chemical reactions, such as the browning of an avocado or the spark of the flame. In a modernized and urban environment, these composites sometimes manifest as synthetics.

Chemists have taken over from the alchemists, and the world teems with newly assembled and rearranged elemental composites. This is especially true in cities.

I see these combinations and recombinations every day in my city and in the local urban ecosystem. Life finds a way to be fruitful, even in the cement desert. Plants grow. Animals live and die feral. The population density does not hide but rather enhances the the spirit of nature and its crew of spirits. A city is just one more biosphere.

Nature spirits exist where there is life. Life exists everywhere in a city, from the dandelion poking out of a crack in the sidewalk to the people walking over it and the birds flying around tall buildings. Any ecosystem falters when there are imbalances, such as when animals move in without the presence of their natural enemies.

Urban ecosystems in particular have become both injured ecosystem and diseased organisms. Their tight spaces are packed with infections of people spewing more waste than the air and water can handle. Despite this, the poison belongs to and comes from nature originally, just as all synthetics originate in an organic source.

The earth can't be destroyed, although the living creatures on it can. Nature lives in the city, because nature and mother earth are eternal, omnipresent, and ultimately will correct for the misbehaviors of their children.

No matter how old, a city is no more than a blip on the face of geological history.

The Dynamic Urban Environment

This duel role as ecosystem and organism causes there to be a spin on the urban environment. A small universe springs to life, filled to the brim with the elemental spirits behind compounds and composites. In their humming motion and fluid density, combined with human motion and emotion, they form ley lines in the ground and overhead strike up a persona known as the city spirit. Each and every one of the elements carries within it some element of the wild.

Cement does not seal away spirits of the land. Steel only repels the sidhe. More than just dandelions work their way through the cracks in a sidewalk. The old gods, with renewed worship, live in urban centers and adapt to new forms. The post office belongs to Hermes or Mercury. Athena lives at city hall, sometimes dressing herself in the outfit of Lady Liberty.

It's entirely possible to connect with nature spirits even as traffic roars past. When walking down a city street sometime, stop to inspect your own shoes and the sidewalk beneath them. Nature lives there, too.

Think about the sidewalk. Sand poured with water makes concrete, so directly beneath your feet lives a spirit of earth, compounded with a very spirit of water. Together these spirits form a new construct that supports you and gives you a comfortable and safe place to walk or a place to bike or skate. Sink your mind into that concrete.

Feel the movement of each molecule. Ask the sand where it came from, and pay attention to what images come to your mind

Expand communications into the geography of the city. Major cities usually have a fresh water source, such as a river or lake. These bodies harbor some of the stronger nature spirits known, and they easily accessed when you walk along the banks of the river, dipping in a toe or finger and spending some time just listening to waves and wind.

The music of water tells beautiful spirit-stories. It is well worth paying attention to the motion and sounds of a stream or the wash of a lake. These rhythms can show how the land you live on was formed and can open you to the secrets of your city.

City Spirits, Mine and Yours

The water spirit of my city is the Mississippi River. I have walked along the banks of this river, making myself known to it. I know the sounds it makes during spring and winter, and I love the muddy smell of it.

In order to know other bodies of water, spend time with them and learn the history of the area. What happened in a particular puddle? How does this affect your perception of the water? What needs, such as litter pick up, does the water have? Find out from the water itself how to develop a relationship.

Some people like to bring offerings to the land masses and to the water bodies of their homes. It's a lovely sentiment, but there are problems with making physical offerings, particularly in water. Even small debris can contribute to clogging and other damage to a stream or lake or other ecosystem. It can also feed aggressive algae that doesn't belong in the body of water and that can harm other life.

Far safer is to make offering of prayer or song, or to gift your energy to the water through caring for it. If you want to make a gift of yourself, direct strong feelings such as admiration or love for the land into a chi ball to sink into the water or into the land. Without clean, fresh water, plants die, reservoirs run dry, and the secondary source of life in the urban world operates with much more difficulty.

Even paper-pushing offices have water coolers and rest rooms, while factories must have water for major portions of their processes. Behind every drop of that water is a spirit that ultimately originates from and returns to the oceans beyond the continent.

The Root of the City Spirit

Land dances with water, its bodies are formed by flows of ice from glaciers and ever eroded and reshaped by rivers and lakes. It is the parent of every city spirit. The land came first, before the settlers and before the indigenous people. It came before the amoebas and earthworms that crawl within its soil. After all buildings crumble, after no feet pound a sidewalk and no trains crunch on tracks, the land will remain.

The personality of land may or may not feel friendly toward its residents. Pay attention to your comfort level and to the general demeanor of your neighbors. Notice any difficulties you have grounding. When friends come to visit, notice subtle changes in their behavior.

If a friend seems more talkative or more anxious in your city, or if he or she has unfamiliar mood swings, it could be the influence of the land itself. Make note especially if you see these patterns repeat in different people who do not have contact with one another. Learn the land as you learned the waters. This foundation anchors you in the face of a whirlwind city.

The City Spirit Above

Nature spirits have their manifest seasons too. Every city is still subject to the seasons of the land that it lives on, and these weather and annual patterns routinely affect the daily lives of every living creature and every spirit residing in these closely spaced habitats of concrete, plaster, and steel, regardless of the amount of open land or other natural forms.

This is not to say that all changes in nature spirits come from the effects of the sky, even though weather is sky-borne and has a considerable effect. When winter comes to a city, it's not just people who hide indoors. In the walls of your home, insects will burrow, and in some older homes even rodents make their homes there.

Every year I read a news story about how some animal traditionally associated with a "wild" habitat has made its home in an urban or suburban area. This includes coyotes, rabbits, mountain lions, and deer, who all adapt to city spaces in their own ways, sometimes to the chagrin or outright terror of their human neighbors.

It only makes sense then that the gnomes can fit underneath the basement, or that sylphs less oriented to cold weather might take a liking to vents.

For those who feel more connected to outdoors and space, make your longing known and the spirit of nature will answer you no matter where you live. One particularly morose winter, I asked for some relief to the sense of isolation I felt in my concrete jungle.

The answer to my wish came when I saw a rabbit hopping down the sidewalk in an industrial section of town. I had to laugh. Not just humans choose to live urban, but skittery forest creatures can do so too.

Just like the bunny, I was scrambling and hopping to keep

up and adapt to my concrete surroundings. I felt less alone just knowing that. Afterward, I made it a point simply to spend more time outside. This is how I found that nature spirits exist in wood and steel alike.

The City Mouse Exercise

Acquaintance with nature spirits happens only through deep exposure. If you are lacking the balance of a better awareness of the natural, you should walk outside your home often. If you live inside the city look for the open spaces there and signs of nature. If you are often making a trip to the city because you're in a suburb, you can tap into the city spirit as well by simply focusing your attention when you go there.

Choose the most concrete-clogged area of the city. Imitate the parable about the country mouse visiting the city mouse. Just like the country mouse, look for any sign of life. This includes other people, plants, insects, stray dogs or cats, and so on. This should take very little time. After all, you're on that patch of concrete, aren't you?

The Urban Spirit Connection

Life combined with spirit attracts the incorporeal. All cities have their share of ghost stories, but not all things taken as ghosts are ghosts. I hesitate to refer to these beings that live everywhere as pixies or elves or fairies. While there are common terms, they fail to explain the nature of these spirits and is also not technically correct.

Fairies in their traditionally correct sense are voluntarily incorporeal beings that live in a parallel dimension of reality and are often bigger than human beings and not particularly fond of cities. (Cities have way too many humans for fairies' tastes.)

The beings that interact in cities are of another sort, without a real classification. These beings, being more complex than elementals but not fairy, are animated spirits that do move into the machinery or stir the shadows at odd times of day to give you warning not to walk somewhere.

An unknown author on http://sourceryforge.org, for example, considers traffic lights the home of urban dryads. While I personally disagree with identifying traffic lights with dryads (since dryads are initially tree spirits, and most cities still grow trees), I do agree that traffic lights have living personalities. Those personalities become familiar with cars and their schedules and sometimes conspire, by shining extra red lights that have nothing to do with the complex timing software of large cities, in order to make the drivers of the cars late (or on time) for wherever they're going.

Buses and trains also become enspirited beyond the basic personification human beings assign them. My favorite form of public transportation, the train, requires a conductor, riders, and metro transit police to ensure people pay for their tickets. In my city, the train's personality exudes a quiet, confident hush that encourages people to sit quietly and read.

Buses' personalities are usually linked to their regular drivers. I have a friend who relies on buses for her primary transportation, and she loves to tell the story of how a sympathetic bus driver and her bus seemed to defy space and time to get her to a modeling job on time each day. She even coined her own magical term for this uncanny ability of her bus and its driver: *bus fu*.

Quirky Spirits, Urban History

In sum, each city has its own quirks and its own spirits. Learn the history of the land where you live. Spend time to get to know your city's quirks, its illogical and magical turns in the road, the habitats and essential spirits of sports teams (and their mascots), and the wonderful quality of its public services—its post offices, its transportation systems, its police force, its schools, its emergency squads, etc.

Learn all about your city, and find where its spirits are hidden. Remember that even indoors with the windows shut at the heart of a teeming city, nature surrounds you.

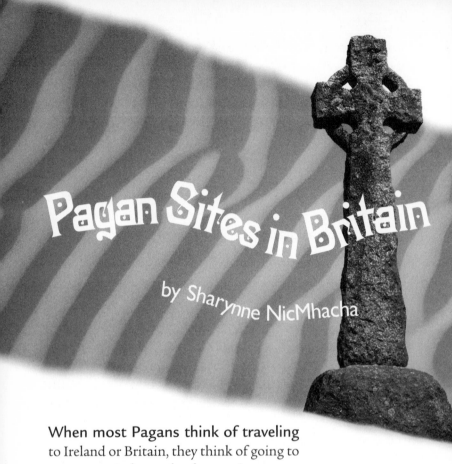

Pagan Sites in Britain

by Sharynne NicMhacha

When most Pagans think of traveling to Ireland or Britain, they think of going to see stone circles and other ancient stone monuments. There are indeed many wonderful and evocative Neolithic sites in the British Isles, ranging in size from large structures like Stonehenge, Avebury, or Callanish to tombs such as the West Kennet Long Barrow, Loughcrew, or Wayland's Smithy.

In many locations, travelers can encounter small local stone circles that are not always marked in travel guides. These sites provide an interesting opportunity to connect with the energy of more intimate locations, as well as an increased chance of finding private time at the site.

There is, however, much more to the Pagan history of Ireland and Britain than these stone monuments. People have been living in the British Isles since about 450,000 BC. For more than 99 percent of that time, people supported themselves by hunting and gathering, and they were quite mobile. The structures they built, for residences and hunting camps, have for the most part not survived (being made out of wood, skins, reeds, or turf). For the first 400,000 of those 450,000 years, we sadly have no evidence of burials or other religious activity that might provide some clue as to the religious and spiritual lives of these people.

There are some artifacts from later eras that the interested Neo-pagan can visit in the fine museums of the British Isles. Many types of stone tools and weapons were produced since earliest times, including hand axes and spears, some of rather beautiful construction. A few artifacts having to do with ancient Pagan burials or religion exist that date to between 25,000 and 16,000 BC. These include ivory and shell jewelry, beads of shale and amber, and some early artwork portraying the animals people depended upon for survival.

In the quiet environment of the museum, you may be surprised at what energies you may pick up from visiting these ancient objects. Not only can we stand in the presence of items actually produced by the Pagan ancestors and begin to understand their way of life, but often we will find ourselves drawn to certain objects that may become teachers or power objects or symbols for us on our path.

Most of the stone circles and passage graves so often visited by modern Pagans were constructed in the last bit of the timeline of human inhabitancy of the British Isles. These arose during the period when farming was introduced and may have resulted from new ways of living, changes in values and society, and an increasing demand for land that resulted from the introduction of agriculture. Although food was more plentiful, other pressures arose from these changes, and the first defended settlements were built at this time. Since we have no written records from this time or before, the only way we can know about religious beliefs is from the objects that were left behind.

In earliest times, grave goods were sparse and included mainly jewelry and pottery vessels. Somewhat later, tools, weapons, pottery, animal bones, and jewelry made of bone, antler, and stone (often serpentine) were found, as well as small stone or chalk balls (possibly fertility objects). After the introduction of metalworking, practical and ritual tools of copper and gold, ritual mace heads of stone, and stone and metal jewelry (including amber, shale, or gold buttons) were buried with the dead.

There is much more to the Pagan history of Ireland and Britain than stone monuments.

While these objects alone cannot tell us what people believed during the vast majority of prehistory, they are amazing gateways to learning about the Pagan past and may provide new personal connections with the old ways. Also, on the rainy days one is likely to encounter on a trip to the British Isles, visiting these sacred objects in the museums provides an interesting and spiritually rich (and dry) activity for the modern Pagan.

Neo-pagans interested in things Celtic often visit the well-known stone circles and tombs. These, however, were built many centuries before the Celts arrived in the British Isles. A few of the pre-Celtic sites—such as Newgrange, Knowth, and Dowth—seem to have been incorporated in later Celtic mythology. There are many actual Celtic Pagan sites that the traveler can explore. In both Ireland and Britain one can visit reconstructions of Iron Age Celtic villages. The Celts tended to worship outdoors or build wooden temples, such as the huge ceremonial structure at Emain Macha. A wonderful visitor center at modern Navan Fort near Armagh tells the story of Emain Macha and provides insight into the beliefs and myths of the Irish Celts.

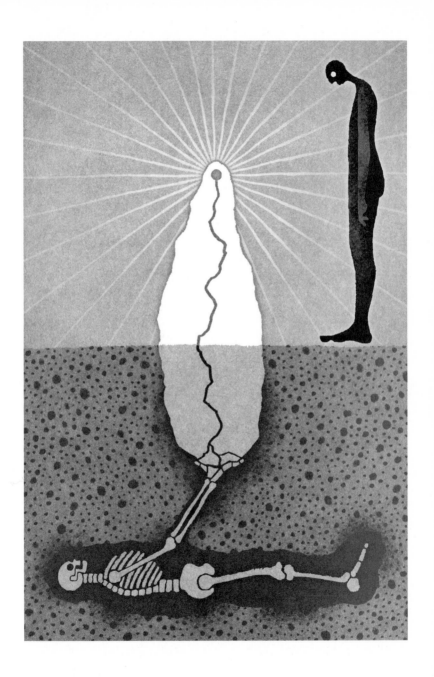

At Loch Tay in Scotland one can visit the Loch Tay Crannog Centre, a reconstruction of an Iron Age Celtic house built on the shores of the loch where many of these sites once existed. There are also innumerable healing wells and springs all over Britain and Ireland. One of the most famous is the healing well of Brigit (originally a Celtic goddess, later a Celtic saint) in Liscannor, County Clare.

In Ireland, one can also visit the actual ritual sites used by the Pagan Irish at the holidays. The Celts observed four sacred feast days: Samhain, Imbolc, Beltane, and Lugnasad. While Imbolc was celebrated within the home, the other three holidays often involved large tribal gatherings. Beltane seems to have been observed at Uisneach, the cosmological center of Ireland; Samhain was celebrated at Tlachtga (now the Hill of Ward), and Lugnasad at several sites, including Tailtiu (modern Telltown). These assembly sites are within a reasonable drive of each other in Meath and Westmeath. All of these locations are enormously "vibey" and interesting, and they are not visited as frequently as the Neolithic sites. You should consider spending time where the ancient Celts used to live and worship to see what sorts of insights and energies you experience.

Reading Celtic myths is another excellent source of travel inspiration. I know both Celtic scholars and spiritual practitioners who have read the Irish tale known as "Cath Maige Tuired" ("The Second Battle of Moytura"), and I have visited many of the sites mentioned in the tale. In this Irish myth, the gods and goddesses (the Tuatha Dé Danann) are involved in a primal struggle with other supernatural beings, and many of the places mentioned in the story can be visited today.

The same is true of the great Irish saga "Táin Bó Cuailgne" ("The Cattle Raid of Cooley"). Imagine standing at the place where the great goddess known as the Mórrígan performed a spell or chant, or where the god Lugh healed his son Cú Chulainn. Good editions of these tales provide an index that tells you where these places are located and gives the modern name of the site. There are also several modern travel books about "sacred" Ireland or Britain that provide similar information. All of these sites are potent places to connect with and honor the gods and goddesses of the Pagan Celts.

There are also mythological sites associated with the land and with the gods and goddesses associated with the sacred land. Sites like the Paps, or Breasts, of Anu (an Irish goddess), and the many place names associated with the folklore figure of the Cailleach (literally, the "Veiled One"), or Hag, are important pilgrimage sites for any devotee of Celtic spirituality.

In addition, in Celtic tradition, rivers were associated with female deities. The River Boyne in Ireland was named for the goddess Boand and the river Shannon for the goddess Sinann. This appears to be an ancient and widespread tradition. In Britain, the Severn was named for the goddess Sabrina and in Cornwall the Tamar was named for Tamara. In Scotland the Clyde was called after the water goddess Clota and the Tay after Tawa. In Scotland are the Rivers Dee (from Dewa, meaning "goddess") and Don (from Dewona, "divine goddess"). Spend time along the banks of these sacred rivers to learn about the goddesses who dwell within their waters.

In Scotland, once lived a group of people we now call the Picts. They were called *Picti* by the Romans, presumably because of their habit of tattooing themselves. They seem to have been known by the term *Pritani* in the ancient British tongue, and *Cruithne* in the early Irish language, both terms meaning "people of the shapes of forms." Perhaps these names also refer to tattoos which the Picts may have sported.

One of the most unique artistic legacies in the British Isles is that of the Picts, who have left us a wonderful variety of symbols carved on to standing stones and engraved on silver jewelry. The jewelry is located in the museums mentioned above, as are some of the stones. Other stones are still located where they once stood, in both the north and south of Scotland in regions once inhabited by the Picts.

The Pictish art style included two types of symbols. One type consisted of representations of animals, birds, and fish that were unique to the British Isles. The other type is called a set abstract symbols by historians, but they must have had important social and religious meaning to the Picts. There are many books and websites that can provide you with a glimpse of this amazing artwork. The Pictish symbols were probably personal or tribal emblems or sigils, some of which may have had spiritual significance.

Another type of interesting inscribed stone exists in Ireland. These are the ogham stones (pronounced "ah-gum'" in Old Irish, or "oe-um" in modern Gaelic). Ogham was a form of writing developed by the Irish in the first few centuries AD. The mythological tradition states that it invented by the god Ogma, who was a skilled warrior and poet. Ogham writing consists of a number of small straight lines, either horizontal or diagonal, which cross or are written on either side of a longer vertical line. Most of the symbols appear to be memorial stones or territory markers, although some of the myths and texts mention ogham being carved on to pieces of wood to send messages or even help student poets remember poems.

There are several types of ogham—i.e., sets of names and meanings associated with each of the letters of the ogham alphabet. The most famous and detailed is associated with types of trees. Some of these are riddles or kennings that the master-poet may have posed to poetic students to help them remember the names of the letters and perhaps associated mystical lore. You can visit the ogham stones in the museums or in fields or on hill-tops where they were raised centuries ago. You can even visit ogham stones up close at University College in Cork, Ireland, in a hallway attached to one of the main buildings.

What about Glastonbury and the myths associated with Avalon? This site has probably attracted more attention and speculation than almost any other connected with Celtic lore. While modern theories about ley lines and zodiacal figures have become attached to the place (creative theories of early occultists not likely having much to do with the original symbolism of the site), Glastonbury is a fascinating place. Certain aspects of its legend do seem to reflect Celtic mythological symbolism.

One of the archetypal locations of the Celtic otherworld was on a sacred island. Interestingly, Glastonbury Tor was once sur-rounded by water. Sacred wells and springs were highly vener-ated by the Celts. The sacred springs in Glastonbury are ancient, and this water supply does not diminish in times of drought. Springs are associated with the colors red and white, which were prominent otherworld colors in Celtic mythological symbolism. The word "Avalon" itself (wherever the site was located) meant "Place of Divine Apple Trees"; the apple tree was a symbol of pas-sage to the otherworld in Celtic tradition.

In addition to the Tor and Chalice Well, Glastonbury Abbey is well worth visiting. It is a highly charged site whose energy must certainly derive from pre-Christian veneration as well as later medieval activity. There is in also in Glastonbury a visitor center that can provide historical information about the Celtic settlements there. Reading about the Celtic mythological ele-ments in Arthurian legend can provide a fascinating and enrich-ing experience when visiting Glastonbury. Celtic mythological symbolism is primarily found only in a small number of early Arthurian sources (prior to Geoffrey of Monmouth). The later tales are products of pan-European storytelling innovations and medieval Christian traditions.

And what about witchcraft? Sorceresses and female magicians are mentioned in several early Irish and British sources. There is also a large body of Irish and Scottish folk magic that many Neo-pagans enjoy exploring.

Still, there seems to be no indications of organized witch-groups or covens in any era, and this concept (like so many others) is probably the invention of churchmen, Inquisitors, and political leaders who feared the organization of magical practitioners (which was perceived as potentially more dangerous than individuals acting alone).

Neo-pagans can learn about folk witchcraft and magical traditions at folk museums, visitor centers, and larger museums in Ireland and Britain. For example, Cornwall boasts a Witch Museum (as well as numerous stone circles, holed stones, and the remains of both Celtic and pre-Celtic settlements). The Scottish museum in Edinburgh has several excellent exhibits of objects associated with Witches and folk magic, including beautiful healing charm stones of polished crystal and set in silver. There is also a fountain dedicated to the people accused of witchcraft in Scotland in the courtyard of Edinburgh Castle.

Whether you wish to learn about modern witchcraft traditions or the indigenous folk magic of the British Isles, folk life centers and occult stores can help you in your pursuit.

Enjoy the stone circles that will undoubtedly crop up as you walk the path of the old ones, but also take time to explore other sources of wisdom and of magical experience that can bring to light the rich Pagan traditions and heritage of Ireland and the British Isles.

Almanac Section

spring 2006 – spring 2007

spring 2006 – spring 2007

spring 2006 – spring 2007

spring 2007

The days & the nights, the Moon & the stars, the colors & the energies, & all the latest Wiccan/Pagan news—the yearly almanac gives you everything you need to get you through this heady astrological year

With news items written by Jennifer Cobb

What's Listed in the Almanac
(and How to Use It)

In these listings you will find the date, lunar phase, Moon sign, color, and magical influence for the day.

The Day

Each day is ruled by a planet that possesses specific magical influences:

Monday (Moon): Peace, sleep, healing, compassion, friends, psychic awareness, purification, and fertility.

Tuesday (Mars): Passion, sex, courage, aggression, and protection.

Wednesday (Mercury): The conscious mind, study, travel, divination, and wisdom.

Thursday (Jupiter): Expansion, money, prosperity, and generosity.

Friday (Venus): Love, friendship, reconciliation, and beauty.

Saturday (Saturn): Longevity, exorcism, endings, homes, and houses.

Sunday (Sun): Healing, spirituality, success, strength, and protection.

The Lunar Phase

The lunar phase is important in determining the best times for magic.

The Waxing Moon (from the New Moon to the Full) is the ideal time for magic to draw things toward you.

The Full Moon is the time of greatest power.

The Waning Moon (from the Full Moon to the New) is a time for study, meditation, and little magical work (except magic designed to banish harmful energies).

The Moon's Sign

The Moon continuously "moves" through the zodiac, from Aries to Pisces. Each sign possesses its own significance:

Aries: Good for initiating things, but lacks staying power and quickly passes. People tend to be argumentative and assertive.

Taurus: Things begun now are lasting, tend to increase in value, and are hard to change. Appreciation for beauty and sensory experience.

Gemini: Things begun now are easily changed by outside influence. Time for shortcuts, communication, games, and fun.

Cancer: Stimulates emotional rapport between people. Pinpoints need, supports growth and nurturance. Tends to domestic concerns.

Leo: Draws emphasis to the self, to central ideas or institutions, away from connections with others and emotional needs. People tend to be melodramatic.

Virgo: Favors accomplishment of details and commands from higher up. Focuses on health, hygiene, and daily schedules.

Libra: Favors cooperation, social activities, beautification of surroundings, balance, and partnership.

Scorpio: Increases awareness of psychic power. Precipitates psychic crises and ends connections thoroughly. People tend to brood and become secretive.

Sagittarius: Encourages flights of imagination and confidence. This is an adventurous, philosophical, and athletic Moon sign. Favors expansion and growth.

Capricorn: Develops strong structure. Focus on traditions, responsibilities, and obligations. A good time to set boundaries and rules.

Aquarius: Rebellious energy. Time to break habits and make abrupt change. Personal freedom and individuality is the focus.

Pisces: The focus is on dreaming, nostalgia, intuition, and psychic impressions. A good time for spiritual or philanthropic activities.

Color and Incense

The colors for the day are based on information from *Personal Alchemy* by Amber Wolfe, and relate to the planet that rules each day. This information can be taken into consideration along with other factors when blending magic into mundane life.

Time Changes

The times and dates of astrological phenomena in this almanac are based on Eastern Standard Time (EST) and Eastern Daylight Time (EDT). If you live outside the Eastern Time Zone, or in a place that does not use Daylight Saving Time, adjust your times:

Central Standard Time: Subtract one hour.

Mountain Standard Time: Subtract two hours.

Pacific Standard Time: Subtract three hours.

Alaska/Hawaii: Subtract five hours.

Areas that have no Daylight Saving Time: Subtract an extra hour from the time given. Daylight Saving Time runs from April 2, 2006, to October 29, 2006, and begins again March 11, 2007.

Key to Astrological Signs

Planets		Signs	
☉	Sun	♈	Aries
♃	Jupiter	♉	Taurus
☽	Moon	♊	Gemini
♄	Saturn	♋	Cancer
☿	Mercury	♌	Leo
♅	Uranus	♍	Virgo
♀	Venus	♎	Libra
♆	Neptune	♏	Scorpio
♂	Mars	♐	Sagittarius
♇	Pluto	♑	Capricorn
		♒	Aquarius
		♓	Pisces

Festivals and Holidays

Festivals are listed throughout the year. The exact dates of many of these ancient festivals are difficult to determine; prevailing data has been used.

2006–2007 Sabbats and Full Moons

March 20, 2006	Ostara (Spring Equinox)
April 13	Full Moon 12:40 pm
May 1	Beltane
May 13	Full Moon 2:51 am
June 11	Full Moon 2:03 pm
June 21	Litha (Summer Solstice)
July 10	Full Moon 11:02 pm
August 1	Lammas
August 9	Full Moon 6:54 am
September 7	Full Moon 2:42 pm
September 23	Mabon (Fall Equinox)
October 6	Full Moon 11:13 pm
October 31	Samhain
November 5	Full Moon 7:58 am
December 4	Full Moon 7:25 pm
December 21	Yule (Winter Solstice)
January 3, 2007	Full Moon 8:57 am
February 2	Imbolc
February 2	Full Moon 12:45 am
March 3	Full Moon 6:17 pm
March 20	Ostara (Spring Equinox)

March 2006

March 20

Ostara · Spring Equinox · Int'l Astrology Day
Waning Moon
Color: Silver

Moon Sign: Scorpio
Moon Phase: Third Quarter
Moon enters Sagittarius 3:43 am

March 21

Juarez Day (Mexican)
Waning Moon
Color: White

Moon Sign: Sagittarius
Moon Phase: Third Quarter

March 22

Hilaria (Roman)
Waning Moon
Color: Topaz

Moon Sign: Sagittarius
Moon Phase: Fourth Quarter 2:10 pm
Moon enters Capricorn 10:36 am

March 23

Pakistan Day
Waning Moon
Color: Crimson

Moon Sign: Capricorn
Moon Phase: Fourth Quarter

March 24

Day of Blood (Roman)
Waning Moon
Color: White

Moon Sign: Capricorn
Moon Phase: Fourth Quarter
Moon enters Aquarius 2:21 pm

March 25

Tichborne Dole (English)
Waning Moon
Color: Indigo

Moon Sign: Aquarius
Moon Phase: Fourth Quarter

March 26 ☉

Prince Kuhio Day (Hawaiian)
Waning Moon
Color: Orange

Moon Sign: Aquarius
Moon Phase: Fourth Quarter
Moon enters Pisces 3:33 pm

March 27

Smell the Breezes Day (English)
Waning Moon
Color: Ivory

Moon Sign: Pisces
Moon Phase: Fourth Quarter

March 28

Oranges and Lemons Service (English)
Waning Moon
Color: Scarlet

Moon Sign: Pisces
Moon Phase: Fourth Quarter
Moon enters Aries 3:31 pm

Tuesday

☿

March 29

St. Eustace's Day
Waning Moon
Color: Brown

Moon Sign: Aries
Moon Phase: New Moon 5:15 am

Wednesday

♃

March 30

Seward's Day (Alaskan)
Waxing Moon
Color: White

Moon Sign: Aries
Moon Phase: First Quarter
Moon enters Taurus 4:00 pm

Thursday

♀

March 31

The Borrowed Days (European)
Waxing Moon
Color: Purple

Moon Sign: Taurus
Moon Phase: First Quarter

Friday

April 2006

Naked Bikers Protest Car Culture

Hundreds of bicyclists wanted to "bare" the facts about oil dependency and the overuse of cars in England and Spain, so they staged a protest called the "World Naked Bike Ride 2005." On June 17, cyclists rode naked through downtown Madrid, appealing for more bike lanes—a move they said would reduce car-related bicycle accidents. In London, activists rode past Big Ben, Piccadilly Circus, and Covent Garden carrying banners reading: "Oil is not a bare necessity but a crude obses-sion." Another cyclist was naked, but for his beliefs. On his back he had painted "No Fumes" and an arrow pointing downward.

April 1	♄
April Fools' Day	Moon Sign: Taurus
Waxing Moon	Moon Phase: First Quarter
Color: Gray	Moon enters Gemini 6:49 pm

April 2	☉
Daylight Saving Time begins	Moon Sign: Gemini
Waxing Moon	Moon Phase: First Quarter
Color: Amber	

☽

Thirteenth Day Out (Iranian)
Waxing Moon
Color: Silver

April 3

Moon Sign: Gemini
Moon Phase: First Quarter

♂

Megalesia (Roman)
Waxing Moon
Color: Red

April 4

Moon Sign: Gemini
Moon Phase: First Quarter
Moon enters Cancer 2:15 am

☿

Tomb-Sweeping Day (Chinese)
Waxing Moon
Color: Yellow

April 5

Moon Sign: Cancer
Moon Phase: Second Quarter 8:01 am

♃

Chakri Day (Thai)
Waxing Moon
Color: Green

April 6

Moon Sign: Cancer
Moon Phase: Second Quarter
Moon enters Leo 12:25 pm

♀

Festival of Pure Brightness (Chinese)
Waxing Moon
Color: Coral

April 7

Moon Sign: Leo
Moon Phase: Second Quarter

♄

Buddha's Birthday
Waxing Moon
Color: Blue

April 8

Moon Sign: Leo
Moon Phase: Second Quarter

☉

Palm Sunday
Waxing Moon
Color: Orange

April 9

Moon Sign: Leo
Moon Phase: Second Quarter
Moon enters Virgo 12:58 am

April 10 ☽

The Tenth of April (English)
Waxing Moon
Color: Lavender

Moon Sign: Virgo
Moon Phase: Second Quarter

April 11 ♂

Heroes' Day (Costa Rican)
Waxing Moon
Color: White

Moon Sign: Virgo
Moon Phase: Second Quarter
Moon enters Libra 1:46 pm

April 12 ☿

Cerealia (Roman)
Waxing Moon
Color: Brown

Moon Sign: Libra
Moon Phase: Second Quarter

April 13 ♃

Passover begins · Thai New Year
Waxing Moon
Color: Crimson

Moon Sign: Libra
Moon Phase: Full Moon 12:40 pm

April 14 ♀

Good Friday
Waning Moon
Color: Pink

Moon Sign: Libra
Moon Phase: Third Quarter
Moon enters Scorpio 1:08 am

April 15 ♄

Plowing Festival (Chinese)
Waning Moon
Color: Indigo

Moon Sign: Scorpio
Moon Phase: Third Quarter

April 16 ☉

Easter
Waning Moon
Color: Yellow

Moon Sign: Scorpio
Moon Phase: Third Quarter
Moon enters Sagittarius 10:19 am

☽ April 17

Yayoi Matsuri (Japanese)
Waning Moon
Color: Gray

Moon Sign: Sagittarius
Moon Phase: Second Quarter

♂ April 18

Flower Festival (Japanese)
Waning Moon
Color: Scarlet

Moon Sign: Sagittarius
Moon Phase: Second Quarter
Moon enters Capricorn 5:13 pm

☿ April 19

Passover ends
Waning Moon
Color: White

Moon Sign: Capricorn
Moon Phase: Third Quarter

♃ April 20

Drum Festival (Japanese)
Waning Moon
Color: Purple

Moon Sign: Capricorn
Moon Phase: Fourth Quarter 11:28 pm
Moon enters Aquarius 9:56 pm

♀ April 21

Orthodox Good Friday
Waning Moon
Color: Rose

Moon Sign: Aquarius
Moon Phase: Fourth Quarter

♄ April 22

Earth Day
Waning Moon
Color: Brown

Moon Sign: Aquarius
Moon Phase: Fourth Quarter

☉ April 23

Orthodox Easter · St. George's Day (English)
Waning Moon
Color: Gold

Moon Sign: Aquarius
Moon Phase: Fourth Quarter
Moon enters Pisces 12:43 am

April 24

St. Mark's Eve
Waning Moon
Color: Ivory

☽

Moon Sign: Pisces
Moon Phase: Fourth Quarter

April 25

Robigalia (Roman)
Waning Moon
Color: Black

♂

Moon Sign: Pisces
Moon Phase: Fourth Quarter
Moon enters Aries 2:12 am

April 26

Arbor Day
Waning Moon
Color: Topaz

☿

Moon Sign: Aries
Moon Phase: Fourth Quarter

April 27

Humabon's Conversion (Filipino)
Waning Moon
Color: Turquoise

♃

Moon Sign: Aries
Moon Phase: New Moon 3:44 pm
Moon enters Taurus 3:27 am

April 28

Floralia (Roman)
Waxing Moon
Color: White

♀

Moon Sign: Taurus
Moon Phase: First Quarter

April 29

Green Day (Japanese)
Waxing Moon
Color: Blue

♄

Moon Sign: Taurus
Moon Phase: First Quarter
Moon enters Gemini 5:58 am

April 30

Walpurgis Night · May Eve
Waxing Moon
Color: Orange

☉

Moon Sign: Gemini
Moon Phase: First Quarter

Villagers Besieged by Pagans

Residents of Avebury have increasingly felt "under siege" when groups of Pagans come to Avebury to celebrate festivals during holy days. They are urging the National Trust to take stronger action to deal with travelers who camp in the village's tourist parking lot. Since 1985, when police cut off access to Stonehenge at the Summer Solstice, Avebury has become more popular as a celebratory destination. Avebury has no permanent washroom facilities, so some fear that unsanitary conditions will lead to illness. Richard Henderson, property manager for the National Trust at Avebury, said that discussions with the parish council were progressing and solutions would soon be found.

News Item

Ancient Beer Beat Illness

An analysis of ancient Nubian bones from Sudan has revealed traces of the antibiotic tetracycline, thought to have come from ancient brewed beer. Tetracycline is today used to treat ailments ranging from acne to urinary tract infections. Anthropologists believe that the ancient tetracycline came from beer made with grain that was contaminated with the bacteria streptomycedes, which produces tetracycline. Ancient Egyptian texts document the use of beer to treat gum disease, dress wounds, and even fumigate against parasites. Anthropologists also believe that tetracycline protected the Nubians from bone infections.

May 2006

May 1 ☽
Monday

Beltane · May Day
Waxing Moon
Color: Gray

Moon Sign: Gemini
Moon Phase: First Quarter
Moon enters Cancer 11:17 am

May 2 ♂
Tuesday

Big Kite Flying (Japanese)
Waxing Moon
Color: Red

Moon Sign: Cancer
Moon Phase: First Quarter

May 3 ☿
Wednesday

Holy Cross Day
Waxing Moon
Color: Yellow

Moon Sign: Cancer
Moon Phase: First Quarter
Moon enters Leo 8:18 pm

May 4 ♃
Thursday

Bona Dea (Roman)
Waxing Moon
Color: Purple

Moon Sign: Leo
Moon Phase: First Quarter

May 5 ♀
Friday

Cinco de Mayo (Mexican)
Waxing Moon
Color: Pink

Moon Sign: Leo
Moon Phase: Second Quarter 1:13 am

May 6 ♄
Saturday

Martyrs' Day (Lebanese)
Waxing Moon
Color: Indigo

Moon Sign: Leo
Moon Phase: Second Quarter
Moon enters Virgo 8:20 am

May 7 ☉
Sunday

Pilgrimage of St. Nicholas (Italian)
Waxing Moon
Color: Yellow

Moon Sign: Virgo
Moon Phase: Second Quarter

☽ **May 8**

Liberation Day (French)
Waxing Moon
Color: Lavender

Moon Sign: Virgo
Moon Phase: Second Quarter
Moon enters Libra 9:10 pm

♂ **May 9**

Lemuria (Roman)
Waxing Moon
Color: White

Moon Sign: Libra
Moon Phase: Second Quarter

☿ **May 10**

First Day of Bird Week (Japanese)
Waxing Moon
Color: Brown

Moon Sign: Libra
Moon Phase: Second Quarter

♃ **May 11**

Ukai Season Opens (Japanese)
Waxing Moon
Color: Green

Moon Sign: Libra
Moon Phase: Second Quarter
Moon enters Scorpio 8:24 am

♀ **May 12**

Florence Nightingale's Birthday
Waxing Moon
Color: Rose

Moon Sign: Scorpio
Moon Phase: First Quarter

♄ **May 13**

Pilgrimage to Fatima (Portuguese)
Waxing Moon
Color: Gray

Moon Sign: Scorpio
Moon Phase: Full Moon 2:51 am
Moon enters Sagittarius 4:56 pm

☉ **May 14**

Mother's Day
Waning Moon
Color: Gold

Moon Sign: Sagittarius
Moon Phase: Third Quarter

May 15 ☽

Festival of St. Dympna (Belgian)
Waning Moon
Color: White

Moon Sign: Sagittarius
Moon Phase: Third Quarter
Moon enters Capricorn 10:59 pm

May 16 ♂

St. Honoratus' Day
Waning Moon
Color: Black

Moon Sign: Capricorn
Moon Phase: Third Quarter

May 17 ☿

Norwegian Independence Day
Waning Moon
Color: Topaz

Moon Sign: Capricorn
Moon Phase: Third Quarter

May 18 ♃

Las Piedras Day (Uruguayan)
Waning Moon
Color: Turquoise

Moon Sign: Capricorn
Moon Phase: Third Quarter
Moon enters Aquarius 3:19 am

May 19 ♀

Pilgrimage to Treguier (French)
Waning Moon
Color: Coral

Moon Sign: Aquarius
Moon Phase: Third Quarter

May 20 ♄

Pardon of the Singers (British)
Waning Moon
Color: Blue

Moon Sign: Aquarius
Moon Phase: Fourth Quarter 5:20 am
Moon enters Pisces 6:39 am

May 21 ☉

Victoria Day (Canadian)
Waning Moon
Color: Amber

Moon Sign: Pisces
Moon Phase: Fourth Quarter

☽ **May 22**

Heroes' Day (Sri Lankan)
Waning Moon
Color: Silver

Moon Sign: Pisces
Moon Phase: Fourth Quarter
Moon enters Aries 9:24 am

♂ **May 23**

Tubilustrium (Roman)
Waning Moon
Color: Gray

Moon Sign: Aries
Moon Phase: Fourth Quarter

☿ **May 24**

Culture Day (Bulgarian)
Waning Moon
Color: White

Moon Sign: Aries
Moon Phase: Fourth Quarter
Moon enters Taurus 12:00 pm

♃ **May 25**

Lady Godiva's Day
Waning Moon
Color: Crimson

Moon Sign: Taurus
Moon Phase: Fourth Quarter

♀ **May 26**

Pepys' Commemoration (English)
Waning Moon
Color: Purple

Moon Sign: Taurus
Moon Phase: Fourth Quarter
Moon enters Gemini 3:19 pm

♄ **May 27**

St. Augustine of Canterbury's Day
Waning Moon
Color: Brown

Moon Sign: Gemini
Moon Phase: New Moon 1:25 am

☉ **May 28**

St. Germain's Day
Waxing Moon
Color: Orange

Moon Sign: Gemini
Moon Phase: First Quarter
Moon enters Cancer 8:33 pm

May 29

☽

Memorial Day (observed)
Waxing Moon
Color: Ivory

Moon Sign: Cancer
Moon Phase: First Quarter

May 30

♂

Radunitsa (Belarussian)
Waxing Moon
Color: Maroon

Moon Sign: Cancer
Moon Phase: First Quarter

May 31

☿

Flowers of May
Waxing Moon
Color: Yellow

Moon Sign: Cancer
Moon Phase: First Quarter
Moon enters Leo 4:51 am

News Item

Police Receive Multifaith Ministering

Police officers in the Thames Valley in England will soon be able to seek, regardless of their faith, official spiritual support. Force chaplain, the Reverend Mark Badger, has been handed the task of creating a new multifaith team to provide a listening ear for all in the force. Rev. Badger said: "I'm here to support officers and staff of all faiths. People working in the police service face urgent, important, and demanding situations every day and I think there's a real need for them to be supported in as many ways as possible." Badger has approached clergy of different faiths around the country and has received commitment from Buddhist, Pagan, Christian, and Muslim representatives.

June 2006

♃

National Day (Tunisian)
Waxing Moon
Color: Turquoise

June 1

Moon Sign: Leo
Moon Phase: First Quarter

♀

Shavuot
Waxing Moon
Color: White

June 2

Moon Sign: Leo
Moon Phase: First Quarter
Moon enters Virgo 4:17 pm

♄

Memorial to Broken Dolls (Japanese)
Waxing Moon
Color: Indigo

June 3

Moon Sign: Virgo
Moon Phase: Second Quarter 7:06 pm

☉

Full Moon Day (Burmese)
Waxing Moon
Color: Orange

June 4

Moon Sign: Virgo
Moon Phase: Second Quarter

June 5 ☽

Constitution Day (Danish)
Waxing Moon
Color: Gray

Moon Sign: Virgo
Moon Phase: Second Quarter
Moon enters Libra 5:08 am

June 6 ♂

Swedish Flag Day
Waxing Moon
Color: White

Moon Sign: Libra
Moon Phase: Second Quarter

June 7 ☿

St. Robert of Newminster's Day
Waxing Moon
Color: Brown

Moon Sign: Libra
Moon Phase: Second Quarter
Moon enters Scorpio 4:41 pm

June 8 ♃

St. Medard's Day (Belgian)
Waxing Moon
Color: Crimson

Moon Sign: Scorpio
Moon Phase: Second Quarter

June 9 ♀

Vestalia (Roman)
Waxing Moon
Color: Pink

Moon Sign: Scorpio
Moon Phase: Second Quarter

June 10 ♄

Time-Observance Day (Chinese)
Waxing Moon
Color: Blue

Moon Sign: Scorpio
Moon Phase: Second Quarter
Moon enters Sagittarius 1:05 am

June 11 ☉

Kamehameha Day (Hawaiian)
Waxing Moon
Color: Gold

Moon Sign: Sagittarius
Moon Phase: Full Moon 2:03 pm

☽ June 12

Independence Day (Filipino)
Waning Moon
Color: Ivory

Moon Sign: Sagittarius
Moon Phase: Third Quarter
Moon enters Capricorn 6:19 am

♂ June 13

St. Anthony of Padua's Day
Waning Moon
Color: Black

Moon Sign: Capricorn
Moon Phase: Third Quarter

☿ June 14

Flag Day
Waning Moon
Color: White

Moon Sign: Capricorn
Moon Phase: Third Quarter
Moon enters Aquarius 9:32 am

♃ June 15

St. Vitus' Day Fires
Waning Moon
Color: Green

Moon Sign: Aquarius
Moon Phase: Third Quarter

♀ June 16

Bloomsday (Irish)
Waning Moon
Color: Rose

Moon Sign: Aquarius
Moon Phase: Third Quarter
Moon enters Pisces 12:05 pm

♄ June 17

Bunker Hill Day
Waning Moon
Color: Gray

Moon Sign: Pisces
Moon Phase: Third Quarter

☉ June 18

Father's Day
Waning Moon
Color: Amber

Moon Sign: Pisces
Moon Phase: Fourth Quarter 10:08 am
Moon enters Aries 2:54 pm

June 19

Juneteenth
Waning Moon
Color: Silver

Moon Sign: Aries
Moon Phase: Fourth Quarter

June 20

Flag Day (Argentinian)
Waning Moon
Color: Gray

Moon Sign: Aries
Moon Phase: Fourth Quarter
Moon enters Taurus 6:23 pm

June 21

Litha · Summer Solstice
Waning Moon
Color: Topaz

Moon Sign: Taurus
Moon Phase: Fourth Quarter

June 22

Rose Festival (English)
Waning Moon
Color: Crimson

Moon Sign: Taurus
Moon Phase: Fourth Quarter
Moon enters Gemini 10:49 pm

June 23

St. John's Eve
Waning Moon
Color: Purple

Moon Sign: Gemini
Moon Phase: Fourth Quarter

June 24

St. John's Day
Waning Moon
Color: Brown

Moon Sign: Gemini
Moon Phase: Fourth Quarter

June 25

⊙

Fiesta of Santa Orosia (Spanish)
Waning Moon
Color: Yellow

Moon Sign: Gemini
Moon Phase: New Moon 12:05 pm
Moon enters Cancer 4:48 am

☽ **June 26**

Pied Piper Day (German)
Waxing Moon
Color: Lavender

Moon Sign: Cancer
Moon Phase: First Quarter

♂ **June 27**

Day of the Seven Sleepers (Islamic)
Waxing Moon
Color: Scarlet

Moon Sign: Cancer
Moon Phase: First Quarter
Moon enters Leo 1:09 pm

☿ **June 28**

Paul Bunyan Day
Waxing Moon
Color: Brown

Moon Sign: Leo
Moon Phase: First Quarter

♃ **June 29**

St. Peter and St. Paul's Day
Waxing Moon
Color: Purple

Moon Sign: Leo
Moon Phase: First Quarter

♀ **June 30**

The Burning of the Three Firs (French)
Waxing Moon
Color: Coral

Moon Sign: Leo
Moon Phase: First Quarter
Moon enters Virgo 12:15 am

July 2006

News Item

Archeologists Sell Stonehenge Replica

Are you searching for a gift for that special Pagan in your life? Well, what if you could buy a life-size replica of Stonehenge? As it happens, one has been put up for sale on eBay. The collection of 171 hand-crafted polystyrene "stones," each five meters tall, was recently listed in the Garden Ornaments section on the website. The life-size model was made in a field near Stonehenge by a team of archeologists for the British television production of *The Ultimate Experience.* Anyone interested in purchasing the model should consider the logistics. You will need a fairly large garden space, as the monumental model takes up more than thirty square meters of space. It also weighs between six and ten tons. (That's a lot of shipping costs.)

July 1   ♄

Climbing Mount Fuji (Japanese)   Moon Sign: Virgo
Waxing Moon   Moon Phase: First Quarter
Color: Gray

July 2   ☉

Heroes' Day (Zambian)   Moon Sign: Virgo
Waxing Moon   Moon Phase: First Quarter
Color: Orange   Moon enters Libra 1:06 pm

☽ July 3

Indian Sun Dance (Native American)
Waxing Moon
Color: White

Moon Sign: Libra
Moon Phase: Second Quarter 12:37 pm

♂ July 4

Independence Day
Waxing Moon
Color: Maroon

Moon Sign: Libra
Moon Phase: Second Quarter

☿ July 5

Tynwald (Nordic)
Waxing Moon
Color: Yellow

Moon Sign: Libra
Moon Phase: Second Quarter
Moon enters Scorpio 1:13 am

♃ July 6

Khao Phansa Day (Thai)
Waxing Moon
Color: Green

Moon Sign: Scorpio
Moon Phase: Second Quarter

♀ July 7

Weaver's Festival (Japanese)
Waxing Moon
Color: White

Moon Sign: Scorpio
Moon Phase: Second Quarter
Moon enters Sagittarius 10:13 am

♄ July 8

St. Elizabeth's Day (Portuguese)
Waxing Moon
Color: Indigo

Moon Sign: Sagittarius
Moon Phase: Second Quarter

☉ July 9

Battle of Sempach Day (Swiss)
Waxing Moon
Color: Amber

Moon Sign: Sagittarius
Moon Phase: Second Quarter
Moon enters Capricorn 3:25 pm

July 10 ☽

Lady Godiva Day (English)
Waxing Moon
Color: Gray

Moon Sign: Capricorn
Moon Phase: Full Moon 11:02 pm

July 11 ♂

Revolution Day (Mongolian)
Waning Moon
Color: Red

Moon Sign: Capricorn
Moon Phase: Third Quarter
Moon enters Aquarius 5:46 pm

July 12 ☿

Lobster Carnival (Nova Scotian)
Waning Moon
Color: Brown

Moon Sign: Aquarius
Moon Phase: Third Quarter

July 13 ♃

Festival of the Three Cows (Spanish)
Waning Moon
Color: Turquoise

Moon Sign: Aquarius
Moon Phase: Third Quarter
Moon enters Pisces 6:59 pm

July 14 ♀

Bastille Day (French)
Waning Moon
Color: Pink

Moon Sign: Pisces
Moon Phase: Third Quarter

July 15 ♄

St. Swithin's Day
Waning Moon
Color: Blue

Moon Sign: Pisces
Moon Phase: Third Quarter
Moon enters Aries 8:39 pm

July 16 ☉

Our Lady of Carmel
Waning Moon
Color: Yellow

Moon Sign: Aries
Moon Phase: Third Quarter

☽ July 17

Rivera Day (Puerto Rican)
Waning Moon
Color: Silver

Moon Sign: Aries
Moon Phase: Fourth Quarter 3:12 pm
Moon enters Taurus 11:44 pm

♂ July 18

Gion Matsuri Festival (Japanese)
Waning Moon
Color: Black

Moon Sign: Taurus
Moon Phase: Fourth Quarter

☿ July 19

Flitch Day (English)
Waning Moon
Color: White

Moon Sign: Taurus
Moon Phase: Fourth Quarter

♃ July 20

Binding of Wreaths (Lithuanian)
Waning Moon
Color: Purple

Moon Sign: Taurus
Moon Phase: Fourth Quarter
Moon enters Gemini 4:38 am

♀ July 21

National Day (Belgian)
Waning Moon
Color: Rose

Moon Sign: Gemini
Moon Phase: Fourth Quarter

♄ July 22

St. Mary Magdalene's Day
Waning Moon
Color: Brown

Moon Sign: Gemini
Moon Phase: Fourth Quarter
Moon enters Cancer 11:28 am

☉ July 23

Mysteries of Santa Cristina (Italian)
Waning Moon
Color: Gold

Moon Sign: Cancer
Moon Phase: Fourth Quarter

July 24 ☽

Pioneer Day (Mormon)
Waning Moon
Color: Ivory

Moon Sign: Cancer
Moon Phase: Fourth Quarter
Moon enters Leo 8:24 pm

July 25 ♂

St. James' Day
Waning Moon
Color: White

Moon Sign: Leo
Moon Phase: New Moon 12:31 am

July 26 ☿

St. Anne's Day
Waxing Moon
Color: Topaz

Moon Sign: Leo
Moon Phase: First Quarter

July 27 ♃

Sleepyhead Day (Finnish)
Waxing Moon
Color: Crimson

Moon Sign: Leo
Moon Phase: First Quarter
Moon enters Virgo 7:36 am

July 28 ♀

Independence Day (Peruvian)
Waxing Moon
Color: Purple

Moon Sign: Virgo
Moon Phase: First Quarter

July 29 ♄

Pardon of the Birds (French)
Waxing Moon
Color: Black

Moon Sign: Virgo
Moon Phase: First Quarter
Moon enters Libra 8:27 pm

July 30 ☉

Micmac Festival of St. Ann
Waxing Moon
Color: Amber

Moon Sign: Libra
Moon Phase: First Quarter

July 31

Weighing of the Aga Khan (Ismaili Muslim)
Waxing Moon
Color: Gray

Moon Sign: Libra
Moon Phase: First Quarter

News Item

Witch School Conjures up Magical Dictionary

The Witch School, which bills itself as the "world's largest Pagan distance-education program," has just mounted a superb web-based resource for Pagans. The online dictionary includes definitions of magical words and words of power, biographies of well-known magical figures, names of modern and ancient deities, and common spells. Now if you encounter a name or term that is unfamiliar, you can go online and find out its origins and meaning—adding to your knowledge of things Pagan and metaphysical. The dictionary is available not just to Pagans, but to any students, writers, reporters, seekers, and even historians who want to learn about the Pagan movement and its people, places, and philosophies. Look it up at http://www.paganwords.com.

August 2006

August 1

Lammas
Waxing Moon
Color: Black

Moon Sign: Libra
Moon Phase: First Quarter
Moon enters Scorpio 9:08 am

August 2

Porcingula (Native American)
Waxing Moon
Color: Yellow

Moon Sign: Scorpio
Moon Phase: Second Quarter 4:46 am

August 3

Drimes (Greek)
Waxing Moon
Color: Green

Moon Sign: Scorpio
Moon Phase: Second Quarter
Moon enters Sagittarius 7:13 pm

August 4

Cook Islands Constitution Celebration
Waxing Moon
Color: White

Moon Sign: Sagittarius
Moon Phase: Second Quarter

August 5

Benediction of the Sea (French)
Waxing Moon
Color: Indigo

Moon Sign: Sagittarius
Moon Phase: Second Quarter

August 6 ☉

Hiroshima Peace Ceremony
Waxing Moon
Color: Orange

Moon Sign: Sagittarius
Moon Phase: Second Quarter
Moon enters Capricorn 1:19 pm

☽ August 7

Republic Day (Ivory Coast)
Waxing Moon
Color: Lavender

Moon Sign: Capricorn
Moon Phase: Second Quarter

♂ August 8

Dog Days (Japanese)
Waxing Moon
Color: Gray

Moon Sign: Capricon
Moon Phase: Second Quarter
Moon enters Aquarius 3:47 am

☿ August 9

Nagasaki Peace Ceremony
Waxing Moon
Color: Brown

Moon Sign: Aquarius
Moon Phase: Full Moon 6:54 am

♃ August 10

St. Lawrence's Day
Waning Moon
Color: Purple

Moon Sign: Aquarius
Moon Phase: Third Quarter
Moon enters Pisces 4:10 am

♀ August 11

Puck Fair (Irish)
Waning Moon
Color: Pink

Moon Sign: Pisces
Moon Phase: Third Quarter

♄ August 12

Fiesta of Santa Clara
Waning Moon
Color: Black

Moon Sign: Pisces
Moon Phase: Third Quarter
Moon enters Aries 4:22 am

☉ August 13

Women's Day (Tunisian)
Waning Moon
Color: Amber

Moon Sign: Aries
Moon Phase: Third Quarter

August 14

Festival at Sassari
Waning Moon
Color: Silver

Moon Sign: Aries
Moon Phase: Third Quarter
Moon enters Taurus 6:00 am

August 15

Assumption Day
Waning Moon
Color: Red

Moon Sign: Taurus
Moon Phase: Fourth Quarter 9:51 pm

August 16

Festival of Minstrels (European)
Waning Moon
Color: Topaz

Moon Sign: Taurus
Moon Phase: Fourth Quarter
Moon enters Gemini 10:07 am

August 17

Feast of the Hungry Ghosts (Chinese)
Waning Moon
Color: Turquoise

Moon Sign: Gemini
Moon Phase: Fourth Quarter

August 18

St. Helen's Day
Waning Moon
Color: Coral

Moon Sign: Gemini
Moon Phase: Fourth Quarter
Moon enters Cancer 5:03 pm

August 19

Rustic Vinalia (Roman)
Waning Moon
Color: Blue

Moon Sign: Cancer
Moon Phase: Fourth Quarter

August 20

Constitution Day (Hungarian)
Waning Moon
Color: Yellow

Moon Sign: Cancer
Moon Phase: Fourth Quarter

August 21

☽

Consualia (Roman)
Waning Moon
Color: Ivory

Moon Sign: Cancer
Moon Phase: Fourth Quarter
Moon enters Leo 2:33 am

August 22

♂

Feast of the Queenship of Mary (English)
Waning Moon
Color: Scarlet

Moon Sign: Leo
Moon Phase: Fourth Quarter

August 23

☿

National Day (Romanian)
Waning Moon
Color: White

Moon Sign: Leo
Moon Phase: New Moon 3:10 pm
Moon enters Virgo 2:08 pm

August 24

♃

St. Bartholomew's Day
Waxing Moon
Color: Crimson

Moon Sign: Virgo
Moon Phase: First Quarter

August 25

♀

Feast of the Green Corn (Native American)
Waxing Moon
Color: Rose

Moon Sign: Virgo
Moon Phase: First Quarter

August 26

♄

Pardon of the Sea (French)
Waxing Moon
Color: Brown

Moon Sign: Virgo
Moon Phase: First Quarter
Moon enters Libra 3:01 am

August 27

☉

Summer Break (English)
Waxing Moon
Color: Gold

Moon Sign: Libra
Moon Phase: First Quarter

August 28

☽

St. Augustine's Day
Waxing Moon
Color: Gray

Moon Sign: Libra
Moon Phase: First Quarter
Moon enters Scorpio 3:56 pm

August 29

♂

St. John's Beheading
Waxing Moon
Color: Maroon

Moon Sign: Scorpio
Moon Phase: First Quarter

August 30

☿

St. Rose of Lima Day (Peruvian)
Waxing Moon
Color: Brown

Moon Sign: Scorpio
Moon Phase: First Quarter

August 31

♃

Unto These Hills Pageant (Cherokee)
Waxing Moon
Color: White

Moon Sign: Scorpio
Moon Phase: Second Quarter 6:56 pm
Moon enters Sagittarius 3:00 am

September 2006

Druids Campaign to Stop Quarrying

On May Day in 2004, Druids gathered at Thornborough Henges to call an end to the quarrying of rock near Ladybridge, one of Britain's largest prehistoric sites. A company called Tarmac has rights to extract sand and gravel from the site. While Tarmac recognizes the sensitive issues surrounding national artifacts and historic sites, they also produce more than 500,000 tons of sand and gravel a year from various quarry sites. Protesters urged National Heritage to undertake a conservation study in order to protect the monument and stop putting profit over history.

♀

Greek New Year
Waxing Moon
Color: Pink

September 1

Moon Sign: Sagittarius
Moon Phase: Second Quarter

♄

St. Mamas' Day
Waxing Moon
Color: Black

September 2

Moon Sign: Sagittarius
Moon Phase: Second Quarter
Moon enters Capricorn 10:34 am

☉

Founder's Day (San Marino)
Waxing Moon
Color: Orange

September 3

Moon Sign: Capricorn
Moon Phase: Second Quarter

September 4
Monday

Labor Day (observed)
Waxing Moon
Color: Lavender

Moon Sign: Capricorn
Moon Phase: Second Quarter
Moon enters: Aquarius 2:15 pm

☾

September 5
Tuesday

First Labor Day (1882)
Waxing Moon
Color: Red

Moon Sign: Aquarius
Moon Phase: Second Quarter

♂

September 6
Wednesday

The Virgin of Remedies (Spanish)
Waxing Moon
Color: Yellow

Moon Sign: Aquarius
Moon Phase: Second Quarter
Moon enters Pisces 2:56 pm

☿

September 7
Thursday

Festival of the Durga (Hindu)
Waxing Moon
Color: Purple

Moon Sign: Pisces
Moon Phase: Full Moon 2:42 pm

♃

September 8
Friday

Birthday of the Virgin Mary
Waning Moon
Color: Coral

Moon Sign: Pisces
Moon Phase: Third Quarter
Moon enters Aries 2:23 pm

♀

September 9
Saturday

Chrysanthemum Festival (Japanese)
Waning Moon
Color: Brown

Moon Sign: Aries
Moon Phase: Third Quarter

♄

September 10
Sunday

Festival of the Poets (Japanese)
Waning Moon
Color: Yellow

Moon Sign: Aries
Moon Phase: Third Quarter
Moon enters Taurus 2:30 pm

☉

September 11

Coptic New Year
Waning Moon
Color: Gray

Moon Sign: Taurus
Moon Phase: Third Quarter

September 12

National Day (Ethiopian)
Waning Moon
Color: Black

Moon Sign: Taurus
Moon Phase: Third Quarter
Moon enters Gemini 4:59 pm

September 13

The Gods' Banquet (Roman)
Waning Moon
Color: White

Moon Sign: Gemini
Moon Phase: Third Quarter

September 14

Holy Cross Day
Waning Moon
Color: Turquoise

Moon Sign: Gemini
Moon Phase: Fourth Quarter 7:15 am
Moon enters Cancer 10:53 pm

September 15

Birthday of the Moon (Chinese)
Waning Moon
Color: Rose

Moon Sign: Cancer
Moon Phase: Fourth Quarter

September 16

Mexican Independence Day
Waning Moon
Color: Blue

Moon Sign: Cancer
Moon Phase: Fourth Quarter

⊙

September 17

Von Steuben's Day
Waning Moon
Color: Gold

Moon Sign: Cancer
Moon Phase: Fourth Quarter
Moon enters Leo 8:15 am

September 18
Dr. Johnson's Birthday
Waning Moon
Color: White

☽

Moon Sign: Leo
Moon Phase: Fourth Quarter

September 19
St. Januarius' Day (Italian)
Waning Moon
Color: Maroon

♂

Moon Sign: Leo
Moon Phase: Fourth Quarter
Moon enters Virgo 8:07 pm

September 20
St. Eustace's Day
Waning Moon
Color: Topaz

☿

Moon Sign: Virgo
Moon Phase: Fourth Quarter

September 21
Christ's Hospital Founder's Day (British)
Waning Moon
Color: Green

♃

Moon Sign: Virgo
Moon Phase: Fourth Quarter

September 22
St. Maurice's Day
Waning Moon
Color: Purple

♀

Moon Sign: Virgo
Moon Phase: New Moon 7:45 am
Moon enters Libra 9:06 am

September 23
Mabon · Fall Equinox · Rosh Hashanah
Waxing Moon
Color: Indigo

♄

Moon Sign: Libra
Moon Phase: First Quarter

September 24
Ramadan begins
Waxing Moon
Color: Amber

☉

Moon Sign: Libra
Moon Phase: First Quarter
Moon enters Scorpio 9:54 pm

September 25

☽

Doll's Memorial Service (Japanese)
Waxing Moon
Color: Ivory

Moon Sign: Scorpio
Moon Phase: First Quarter

September 26

♂

Feast of Santa Justina (Mexican)
Waxing Moon
Color: White

Moon Sign: Scorpio
Moon Phase: First Quarter

September 27

☿

Saints Cosmas and Damian's Day
Waxing Moon
Color: Brown

Moon Sign: Scorpio
Moon Phase: First Quarter
Moon enters Sagittarius 9:16 am

September 28

♃

Confucius' Birthday
Waxing Moon
Color: Crimson

Moon Sign: Sagittarius
Moon Phase: First Quarter

September 29

♀

Michaelmas
Waxing Moon
Color: White

Moon Sign: Sagittarius
Moon Phase: First Quarter
Moon enters Capricorn 6:01 pm

September 30

♄

St. Jerome's Day
Waxing Moon
Color: Gray

Moon Sign: Capricorn
Moon Phase: Second Quarter 7:04 am

October 2006

News Item

The Media Cries "Witch"

The remains of a pony and a headless horse were found in the River Parrett in southwest England by a woman walking her dog. Local media responded with speculation of witchcraft and "suspicious circumstances." With no factual evidence to support such suspicions, media observers reported, the local papers simply sensationalized the story, in order to sell papers and malign local practitioners of Wicca.

October 1   ☉

Armed Forces Day (South Korean)   Moon Sign: Capricorn
Waxing Moon   Moon Phase: Second Quarter
Color: Yellow   Moon enters Aquarius 11:24 pm

October 2

Yom Kippur
Waxing Moon
Color: White

Moon Sign: Aquarius
Moon Phase: Second Quarter

♂

October 3

Moroccan New Year's Day
Waxing Moon
Color: Red

Moon Sign: Aquarius
Moon Phase: Second Quarter

☿

October 4

St. Francis' Day
Waxing Moon
Color: Topaz

Moon Sign: Aquarius
Moon Phase: Second Quarter
Moon enters Pisces 1:33 am

♃

October 5

Republic Day (Portuguese)
Waxing Moon
Color: Purple

Moon Sign: Pisces
Moon Phase: Second Quarter

♀

October 6

Dedication of the Virgin's Crowns (English)
Waxing Moon
Color: Pink

Moon Sign: Pisces
Moon Phase: Full Moon 11:13 pm
Moon enters Aries 1:32 am

♄

October 7

Sukkot begins · Kermesse (German)
Waning Moon
Color: Black

Moon Sign: Aries
Moon Phase: Third Quarter

October 8

Okunchi (Japanese)
Waning Moon
Color: Orange

Moon Sign: Aries
Moon Phase: Third Quarter
Moon enters Taurus 1:04 am

October 9

Columbus Day (observed)
Waning Moon
Color: Lavender

☽

Moon Sign: Taurus
Moon Phase: Third Quarter

October 10

Health Day (Japanese)
Waning Moon
Color: White

♂

Moon Sign: Taurus
Moon Phase: Third Quarter
Moon enters Gemini 2:06 am

October 11

Meditrinalia (Roman)
Waning Moon
Color: Yellow

☿

Moon Sign: Gemini
Moon Phase: Third Quarter

October 12

National Day (Spanish)
Waning Moon
Color: Turquoise

♃

Moon Sign: Gemini
Moon Phase: Third Quarter
Moon enters Cancer 6:21 am

October 13

Sukkot ends
Waning Moon
Color: Rose

♀

Moon Sign: Cancer
Moon Phase: Fourth Quarter 8:25 pm

October 14

Battle Festival (Japanese)
Waning Moon
Color: Indigo

♄

Moon Sign: Cancer
Moon Phase: Fourth Quarter
Moon enters Leo 2:38 pm

October 15

The October Horse (Roman)
Waning Moon
Color: Amber

☉

Moon Sign: Leo
Moon Phase: Fourth Quarter

☽

The Lion Sermon (British)
Waning Moon
Color: Ivory

October 16

Moon Sign: Leo
Moon Phase: Fourth Quarter

♂

Pilgrimage to Paray-le-Monial
Waning Moon
Color: Gray

October 17

Moon Sign: Leo
Moon Phase: Fourth Quarter
Moon enters Virgo 2:15 am

☿

Brooklyn Barbeque
Waning Moon
Color: Brown

October 18

Moon Sign: Virgo
Moon Phase: Fourth Quarter

♃

Our Lord of Miracles Procession (Peruvian)
Waning Moon
Color: Green

October 19

Moon Sign: Virgo
Moon Phase: Fourth Quarter
Moon enters Libra 3:19 pm

♀

Colchester Oyster Feast
Waning Moon
Color: White

October 20

Moon Sign: Libra
Moon Phase: Fourth Quarter

♄

Feast of the Black Christ
Waning Moon
Color: Blue

October 21

Moon Sign: Libra
Moon Phase: Fourth Quarter

☉

Goddess of Mercy Day (Chinese)
Waning Moon
Color: Gold

October 22

Moon Sign: Libra
Moon Phase: New Moon 1:14 am
Moon enters Scorpio 3:54 am

October 23 ☽

Revolution Day (Hungarian)
Waxing Moon
Color: Silver

Moon Sign: Scorpio
Moon Phase: First Quarter

October 24 ♂

United Nations Day · Ramadan ends
Waxing Moon
Color: Scarlet

Moon Sign: Scorpio
Moon Phase: First Quarter
Moon enters Sagittarius 2:53 pm

October 25 ☿

St. Crispin's Day
Waxing Moon
Color: White

Moon Sign: Sagittarius
Moon Phase: First Quarter

October 26 ♃

Quit Rent Ceremony (British)
Waxing Moon
Color: Purple

Moon Sign: Sagittarius
Moon Phase: First Quarter
Moon enters Capricorn 11:47 pm

October 27 ♀

Feast of the Holy Souls
Waxing Moon
Color: Coral

Moon Sign: Capricorn
Moon Phase: First Quarter

October 28 ♄

Ochi Day (Greek)
Waxing Moon
Color: Black

Moon Sign: Capricorn
Moon Phase: First Quarter

October 29 ☉

Daylight Saving Time ends
Waxing Moon
Color: Orange

Moon Sign: Capricorn
Moon Phase: Second Quarter 4:25 pm
Moon enters Aquarius 5:17 am

October 30

Meiji Festival (Japanese)
Waxing Moon
Color: Lavender

Moon Sign: Aquarius
Moon Phase: Second Quarter

October 31

Halloween · Samhain
Waxing Moon
Color: Gray

Moon Sign: Aquarius
Moon Phase: Second Quarter
Moon enters Pisces 9:10 am

News Item

Researchers Find Oldest Art in England

Scientists have confirmed that rock art at Creswell Crags in northeast England are the oldest engravings yet discovered in Britain. Measuring traces of radioactive uranium found in the limestone crust over the engravings, a scientific team from Bristol, Sheffield, and Open universities calculated that the artwork is more than 12,800 years old and was produced during the last Ice Age. The pictographs depict European bison, now extinct from Britain, and other animals and figures. Other artifacts excavated from Creswell's caves have been dated to 13,000–15,000 years old.

November 2006

November 1	☿
All Saints' Day	Moon Sign: Pisces
Waxing Moon	Moon Phase: Second Quarter
Color: White	

November 2	♃
All Souls' Day	Moon Sign: Pisces
Waxing Moon	Moon Phase: Second Quarter
Color: Turquoise	Moon enters Aries 10:46 am

November 3	♀
St. Hubert's Day	Moon Sign: Aries
Waxing Moon	Moon Phase: Second Quarter
Color: White	

November 4	♄
Mischief Night (British)	Moon Sign: Aries
Waxing Moon	Moon Phase: Second Quarter
Color: Blue	Moon enters Taurus 11:05 am

November 5	☉
Guy Fawkes Night (British)	Moon Sign: Taurus
Waxing Moon	Moon Phase: Full Moon 7:58 am
Color: Amber	

November 6

Leonard's Ride (German)
Waning Moon
Color: Lavender

Moon Sign: Taurus
Moon Phase: Third Quarter
Moon enters Gemini 11:46 am

November 7

Mayan Day of the Dead · Election Day
Waning Moon
Color: White

Moon Sign: Gemini
Moon Phase: Third Quarter

November 8

The Lord Mayor's Show (English)
Waning Moon
Color: Brown

Moon Sign: Gemini
Moon Phase: Third Quarter
Moon enters Cancer 2:46 pm

♃

November 9

Lord Mayor's Day (British)
Waning Moon
Color: Purple

Moon Sign: Cancer
Moon Phase: Third Quarter

♀

November 10

Martin Luther's Birthday
Waning Moon
Color: Coral

Moon Sign: Cancer
Moon Phase: Third Quarter
Moon enters Aries 9:34 pm

November 11

Veterans Day
Waning Moon
Color: Indigo

Moon Sign: Leo
Moon Phase: Third Quarter

☉

November 12

Tesuque Feast Day (Native American)
Waning Moon
Color: Orange

Moon Sign: Leo
Moon Phase: Fourth Quarter 12:45 pm

November 13 ☽

Festival of Jupiter (Roman)
Waning Moon
Color: Silver

Moon Sign: Leo
Moon Phase: Fourth Quarter
Moon enters Virgo 8:18 am

November 14 ♂

The Little Carnival (Greek)
Waning Moon
Color: Black

Moon Sign: Virgo
Moon Phase: Fourth Quarter

November 15 ☿

St. Leopold's Day
Waning Moon
Color: White

Moon Sign: Virgo
Moon Phase: Fourth Quarter
Moon enters Libra 9:14 pm

November 16 ♃

St. Margaret of Scotland's Day
Waning Moon
Color: Crimson

Moon Sign: Libra
Moon Phase: Fourth Quarter

November 17 ♀

Queen Elizabeth's Day
Waning Moon
Color: Pink

Moon Sign: Libra
Moon Phase: Fourth Quarter

November 18 ♄

St. Plato's Day
Waning Moon
Color: Gray

Moon Sign: Libra
Moon Phase: Fourth Quarter
Moon enters Scorpio 9:46 am

November 19 ☉

Garifuna Day (Belizian)
Waning Moon
Color: Yellow

Moon Sign: Scorpio
Moon Phase: Fourth Quarter

☽ November 20

Commerce God Ceremony (Japanese)
Waning Moon
Color: Ivory

Moon Sign: Scorpio
Moon Phase: New Moon 5:18 pm
Moon enters Sagittarius 8:15 pm

♂ November 21

Repentance Day (German)
Waxing Moon
Color: Maroon

Moon Sign: Sagittarius
Moon Phase: First Quarter

☿ November 22

St. Cecilia's Day
Waxing Moon
Color: Topaz

Moon Sign: Sagittarius
Moon Phase: First Quarter

♃ November 23

Thanksgiving Day
Waxing Moon
Color: Green

Moon Sign: Sagittarius
Moon Phase: First Quarter
Moon enters Capricorn 4:25 am

♀ November 24

Feast of the Burning Lamps (Egyptian)
Waxing Moon
Color: Rose

Moon Sign: Capricorn
Moon Phase: First Quarter

♄ November 25

St. Catherine of Alexandria's Day
Waxing Moon
Color: Black

Moon Sign: Capricorn
Moon Phase: First Quarter
Moon enters Aquarius 10:41 am

☉ November 26

Festival of Lights (Tibetan)
Waxing Moon
Color: Gold

Moon Sign: Aquarius
Moon Phase: First Quarter

November 27

St. Maximus' Day
Waxing Moon
Color: Gray

Moon Sign: Aquarius
Moon Phase: First Quarter
Moon enters Pisces 3:20 pm

November 28

Day of the New Dance (Tibetan)
Waxing Moon
Color: Red

Moon Sign: Pisces
Moon Phase: Second Quarter 1:29 am

November 29

Tubman's Birthday (Liberian)
Waxing Moon
Color: Brown

Moon Sign: Pisces
Moon Phase: Second Quarter
Moon enters Aries 6:30 pm

November 30

$2\!\!\!\!4$

St. Andrew's Day
Waxing Moon
Color: Purple

Moon Sign: Aries
Moon Phase: Second Quarter

December 2006

News Item

Archeologists Hunt for Hot Baths

A team of archeologists have begun excavating at Groundwell Ridge in Wiltshire, England, in search of ancient hot baths. A Roman villa was discovered at a construction site north of the town in 1996, which led English Heritage and the Swindon Borough Council to work together to buy the land and fund excavations. In 2004, archeologists discovered cold water baths dating back 1,600 years. With recent excavations, they hope to find the location of Roman hot water baths.

♀   **December 1**

Big Tea Party (Japanese)   Moon Sign: Aries
Waxing Moon   Moon Phase: Second Quarter
Color: Coral   Moon enters Taurus 8:26 pm

Friday

♄   **December 2**

Republic Day (Laotian)   Moon Sign: Taurus
Waxing Moon   Moon Phase: Second Quarter
Color: Brown

Saturday

☉   **December 3**

St. Francis Xavier's Day   Moon Sign: Taurus
Waxing Moon   Moon Phase: Second Quarter
Color: Yellow   Moon enters Gemini 10:05 pm

Sunday

December 4

St. Barbara's Day
Waxing Moon
Color: Silver

☽

Moon Sign: Gemini
Moon Phase: Full Moon 7:25 pm

December 5

Eve of St. Nicholas' Day
Waning Moon
Color: Black

♂

Moon Sign: Gemini
Moon Phase: Third Quarter

December 6

St. Nicholas' Day
Waning Moon
Color: White

☿

Moon Sign: Gemini
Moon Phase: Third Quarter
Moon enters Cancer 1:00 am

December 7

Burning the Devil (Guatemalan)
Waning Moon
Color: Turquoise

♃

Moon Sign: Cancer
Moon Phase: Third Quarter

December 8

Feast of the Immaculate Conception
Waning Moon
Color: White

♀

Moon Sign: Cancer
Moon Phase: Third Quarter
Moon enters Leo 6:52 am

December 9

St. Leocadia's Day
Waning Moon
Color: Gray

♄

Moon Sign: Leo
Moon Phase: Third Quarter

December 10

Nobel Day
Waning Moon
Color: Orange

☉

Moon Sign: Leo
Moon Phase: Third Quarter
Moon enters Virgo 4:31 pm

☽ **December 11**

Pilgrimage at Tortugas
Waning Moon
Color: Lavender

Moon Sign: Virgo
Moon Phase: Third Quarter

♂ **December 12**

Fiesta of Our Lady of Guadalupe
Waning Moon
Color: Maroon

Moon Sign: Virgo
Moon Phase: Fourth Quarter 9:32 am

☿ **December 13**

St. Lucy's Day (Swedish)
Waning Moon
Color: Brown

Moon Sign: Virgo
Moon Phase: Fourth Quarter
Moon enters Libra 5:00 am

♃ **December 14**

Warrior's Memorial (Japanese)
Waning Moon
Color: Green

Moon Sign: Libra
Moon Phase: Fourth Quarter

♀ **December 15**

Consualia (Roman)
Waning Moon
Color: Pink

Moon Sign: Libra
Moon Phase: Fourth Quarter
Moon enters Scorpio 5:42 pm

♄ **December 16**

Posadas (Mexican) · Hannukah begins
Waning Moon
Color: Blue

Moon Sign: Scorpio
Moon Phase: Fourth Quarter

☉ **December 17**

Saturnalia (Roman)
Waning Moon
Color: Amber

Moon Sign: Scorpio
Moon Phase: Fourth Quarter

December 18 ☽

Monday

Feast of the Virgin of Solitude
Waning Moon
Color: Gray

Moon Sign: Scorpio
Moon Phase: Fourth Quarter
Moon enters Sagittarius 4:10 am

December 19 ♂

Tuesday

Opalia (Roman)
Waning Moon
Color: Red

Moon Sign: Sagittarius
Moon Phase: Fourth Quarter

December 20 ☿

Wednesday

Commerce God Festival
Waning Moon
Color: Yellow

Moon Sign: Sagittarius
Moon Phase: New Moon 9:01 am
Moon enters Capricorn 11:39 am

December 21 ♃

Thursday

Yule · Winter Solstice
Waxing Moon
Color: Crimson

Moon Sign: Capricorn
Moon Phase: First Quarter

December 22 ♀

Friday

Saints Chaeremon and Ischyrion's Day
Waxing Moon
Color: Coral

Moon Sign: Capricorn
Moon Phase: First Quarter
Moon enters Aquarius 4:49 pm

December 23 ♄

Saturday

Larentalia (Roman) · Hannukah ends
Waxing Moon
Color: Indigo

Moon Sign: Aquarius
Moon Phase: First Quarter

December 24 ☉

Sunday

Christmas Eve
Waxing Moon
Color: Gold

Moon Sign: Aquarius
Moon Phase: First Quarter
Moon enters Pisces 8:43 pm

☽   December 25

Christmas   Moon Sign: Pisces
Waxing Moon   Moon Phase: First Quarter
Color: Ivory

♂   December 26

Kwanzaa begins   Moon Sign: Pisces
Waxing Moon   Moon Phase: First Quarter
Color: Scarlet

☿   December 27

Boar's Head Supper (English)   Moon Sign: Pisces
Waxing Moon   Moon Phase: Second Quarter 9:48 am
Color: Topaz   Moon enters Aries 12:04 am

♃   December 28

Holy Innocents' Day   Moon Sign: Aries
Waxing Moon   Moon Phase: Second Quarter
Color: White

♀   December 29

St. Thomas à Becket's Day   Moon Sign: Aries
Waxing Moon   Moon Phase: Second Quarter
Color: Purple   Moon enters Taurus 3:08 am

♄   December 30

Republic Day (Madagascarian)   Moon Sign: Taurus
Waxing Moon   Moon Phase: Second Quarter
Color: Black

☉   December 31

New Year's Eve   Moon Sign: Taurus
Waxing Moon   Moon Phase: Second Quarter
Color: Yellow   Moon enters Gemini 6:16 am

☽

January 1

Monday

New Year's Day · Kwanzaa ends
Waxing Moon
Color: Gray

Moon Sign: Gemini
Moon Phase: Second Quarter

♂

January 2

Tuesday

First Writing (Japanese)
Waxing Moon
Color: Red

Moon Sign: Gemini
Moon Phase: Second Quarter
Moon enters Cancer 10:14 am

☿

January 3

Wednesday

St. Genevieve's Day
Waxing Moon
Color: Yellow

Moon Sign: Cancer
Moon Phase: Full Moon 8:57 am

♃

January 4

Thursday

Frost Fairs on the Thames
Waning Moon
Color: Green

Moon Sign: Cancer
Moon Phase: Third Quarter
Moon enters Leo 4:14 pm

♀

January 5

Friday

Epiphany Eve
Waning Moon
Color: White

Moon Sign: Leo
Moon Phase: Third Quarter

♄

January 6

Saturday

Epiphany
Waning Moon
Color: Brown

Moon Sign: Leo
Moon Phase: Third Quarter

☉

January 7

Sunday

Rizdvo (Ukrainian)
Waning Moon
Color: Yellow

Moon Sign: Leo
Moon Phase: Third Quarter
Moon enters Virgo 1:18 am

January 8

Midwives' Day
Waning Moon
Color: Lavender

Moon Sign: Virgo
Moon Phase: Third Quarter

♂

January 9

Feast of the Black Nazarene (Filipino)
Waning Moon
Color: White

Moon Sign: Virgo
Moon Phase: Third Quarter
Moon enters Libra 1:15 pm

☿

January 10

Business God's Day (Japanese)
Waning Moon
Color: Brown

Moon Sign: Libra
Moon Phase: Third Quarter

♃

January 11

Carmentalia (Roman)
Waning Moon
Color: Turquoise

Moon Sign: Libra
Moon Phase: Fourth Quarter 7:44 am

♀

January 12

Revolution Day (Tanzanian)
Waning Moon
Color: Pink

Moon Sign: Libra
Moon Phase: Fourth Quarter
Moon enters Scorpio 2:08 am

♄

January 13

Twentieth Day (Norwegian)
Waning Moon
Color: Gray

Moon Sign: Scorpio
Moon Phase: Fourth Quarter

☉

January 14

Feast of the Ass (French)
Waning Moon
Color: Orange

Moon Sign: Scorpio
Moon Phase: Fourth Quarter
Moon enters Sagittarius 1:11 pm

January 15 ☽

Monday

Martin Luther King Jr.'s Birthday (actual & observed)   Moon Sign: Sagittarius
Waning Moon   Moon Phase: Fourth Quarter
Color: White

January 16 ♂

Tuesday

Apprentices' Day   Moon Sign: Sagittarius
Waning Moon   Moon Phase: Fourth Quarter
Color: Blue   Moon enters Capricorn 8:49 pm

January 17 ☿

Wednesday

St. Anthony's Day (Mexican)   Moon Sign: Capricorn
Waning Moon   Moon Phase: Fourth Quarter
Color: Topaz

January 18 ♃

Thursday

Assumption Day   Moon Sign: Capricorn
Waning Moon   Moon Phase: New Moon 11:01 pm
Color: Purple

January 19 ♀

Friday

Kitchen God Feast (Chinese)   Moon Sign: Capricorn
Waning Moon   Moon Phase: First Quarter
Color: Rose   Moon enters Aquarius 1:15 am

January 20 ♄

Saturday

Breadbasket Festival (Portuguese) · Islamic New Year   Moon Sign: Aquarius
Waxing Moon   Moon Phase: First Quarter
Color: Blue

January 21 ☉

Sunday

St. Agnes Day   Moon Sign: Aquarius
Waxing Moon   Moon Phase: First Quarter
Color: Gold   Moon enters Pisces 3:48 am

☽ **January 22**

St. Vincent's Day
Waxing Moon
Color: Silver

Moon Sign: Pisces
Moon Phase: First Quarter

♂ **January 23**

St. Ildefonso's Day
Waxing Moon
Color: Gray

Moon Sign: Pisces
Moon Phase: First Quarter
Moon enters Aries 5:52 am

☿ **January 24**

Alasitas Fair (Bolivian)
Waxing Moon
Color: White

Moon Sign: Aries
Moon Phase: First Quarter

♃ **January 25**

Burns' Night (Scottish)
Waxing Moon
Color: Crimson

Moon Sign: Aries
Moon Phase: Second Quarter 6:01 pm
Moon enters Taurus 8:28 am

♀ **January 26**

Republic Day (Indian)
Waxing Moon
Color: Coral

Moon Sign: Taurus
Moon Phase: Second Quarter

♄ **January 27**

Vogelgruff (Swiss)
Waxing Moon
Color: Indigo

Moon Sign: Taurus
Moon Phase: Second Quarter
Moon enters Gemini 12:10 pm

☉ **January 28**

St. Charlemagne's Day
Waxing Moon
Color: Amber

Moon Sign: Gemini
Moon Phase: Second Quarter

January 29 ☽

Australia Day   Moon Sign: Gemini
Waxing Moon   Moon Phase: Second Quarter
Color: Ivory   Moon enters Cancer 5:16 pm

January 30 ♂

Three Hierarchs' Day (Eastern Orthodox)   Moon Sign: Cancer
Waxing Moon   Moon Phase: Second Quarter
Color: Maroon

January 31 ☿

Independence Day (Nauru)   Moon Sign: Cancer
Waxing Moon   Moon Phase: Second Quarter
Color: Yellow

News Item

Wiccan Priestess Prohibited from Praying

Cynthia Simpson, a Wiccan priestess from Chesterfield County, Virginia, was prohibited from leading the opening prayer at a local county board of supervisors meeting. Officials claimed that her beliefs as a Wiccan were not consistent with Judeo-Christian tradition, but a trial judge ruled that it was unconstitutional to prohibit her from praying. The county has appealed the decision. Ms. Simpson said she plans to appeal the decision of the appeals court if it does not rule in her favor.

February 2007

♃
February 1

St. Brigid's Day (Irish)
Waxing Moon
Color: White

Moon Sign: Cancer
Moon Phase: Second Quarter
Moon enters Leo 12:14 am

♀
February 2

Imbolc · Groundhog Day
Waxing Moon
Color: Purple

Moon Sign: Leo
Moon Phase: Full Moon 12:45 am

♄
February 3

St. Blaise's Day
Waning Moon
Color: Brown

Moon Sign: Leo
Moon Phase: Third Quarter
Moon enters Virgo 9:34 am

☉
February 4

Independence Day (Sri Lankan)
Waning Moon
Color: Orange

Moon Sign: Virgo
Moon Phase: Third Quarter

February 5 ☽

Festival de la Alcaldesa (Italian)
Waning Moon
Color: Gray

Moon Sign: Virgo
Moon Phase: Third Quarter
Moon enters Libra 9:15 pm

February 6 ♂

Bob Marley's Birthday (Jamaican)
Waning Moon
Color: Red

Moon Sign: Libra
Moon Phase: Third Quarter

February 7 ☿

Full Moon Poya (Sri Lankan)
Waning Moon
Color: White

Moon Sign: Libra
Moon Phase: Third Quarter

February 8 ♃

Mass for Broken Needles (Japanese)
Waning Moon
Color: Crimson

Moon Sign: Libra
Moon Phase: Third Quarter
Moon enters Scorpio 10:09 am

February 9 ♀

St. Marion's Day (Lebanese)
Waning Moon
Color: Rose

Moon Sign: Scorpio
Moon Phase: Third Quarter

February 10 ♄

Gasparilla Day (Floridian)
Waning Moon
Color: Blue

Moon Sign: Scorpio
Moon Phase: Fourth Quarter 4:51 am
Moon enters Sagittarius 10:01 pm

February 11 ☉

Foundation Day (Japanese)
Waning Moon
Color: Amber

Moon Sign: Sagittarius
Moon Phase: Fourth Quarter

☽ **February 12**

Lincoln's Birthday (actual)
Waning Moon
Color: Lavender

Moon Sign: Sagittarius
Moon Phase: Fourth Quarter

♂ **February 13**

Parentalia (Roman)
Waning Moon
Color: White

Moon Sign: Sagittarius
Moon Phase: Fourth Quarter
Moon enters Capricorn 6:42 am

☿ **February 14**

Valentine's Day
Waning Moon
Color: Brown

Moon Sign: Capricorn
Moon Phase: Fourth Quarter

♃ **February 15**

Lupercalia (Roman)
Waning Moon
Color: Turquoise

Moon Sign: Capricorn
Moon Phase: Fourth Quarter
Moon enters Aquarius 11:34 am

♀ **February 16**

Fumi-e (Japanese)
Waning Moon
Color: Coral

Moon Sign: Aquarius
Moon Phase: Fourth Quarter

♄ **February 17**

Quirinalia (Roman)
Waning Moon
Color: Indigo

Moon Sign: Aquarius
Moon Phase: New Moon 11:14 am
Moon enters Pisces 1:30 pm

☉ **February 18**

Chinese New Year (boar)
Waxing Moon
Color: Gold

Moon Sign: Pisces
Moon Phase: First Quarter

February 19

Presidents' Day
Waxing Moon
Color: White

☽

Moon Sign: Pisces
Moon Phase: First Quarter
Moon enters Aries 2:06 pm

February 20

Mardi Gras
Waxing Moon
Color: Maroon

♂

Moon Sign: Aries
Moon Phase: First Quarter

February 21

Ash Wednesday
Waxing Moon
Color: Yellow

☿

Moon Sign: Aries
Moon Phase: First Quarter
Moon enters Taurus 3:03 pm

February 22

Caristia (Roman)
Waxing Moon
Color: Green

♃

Moon Sign: Taurus
Moon Phase: First Quarter

February 23

Terminalia (Roman)
Waxing Moon
Color: Pink

♀

Moon Sign: Taurus
Moon Phase: First Quarter
Moon enters Gemini 5:42 pm

February 24

Regifugium (Roman)
Waxing Moon
Color: Gray

♄

Moon Sign: Gemini
Moon Phase: Second Quarter 2:56 am

February 25

St. Walburga's Day
Waxing Moon
Color: Yellow

☉

Moon Sign: Gemini
Moon Phase: Second Quarter
Moon enters Cancer 10:47 pm

☽ **February 26**

Zamboanga Festival (Filipino)
Waxing Moon
Color: Ivory

Moon Sign: Cancer
Moon Phase: Second Quarter

♂ **February 27**

Threepenny Day
Waxing Moon
Color: Black

Moon Sign: Cancer
Moon Phase: Second Quarter

☿ **February 28**

Kalevala Day (Finnish)
Waxing Moon
Color: Topaz

Moon Sign: Cancer
Moon Phase: Second Quarter
Moon enters Leo 6:29 am

News Item

Witchcraft Shown Live on BBC

The BBC's *Africa Live* aired a feature on witchcraft in
Africa. Traditional African spiritual and healing practices were shown to have played a role in rebellions, wars, independence struggles, and political elections. In many parts of Africa, people traditionally consult witch doctors to cure diseases or find a mate. While many of the traditional practices are positive in effect and outcome, there are also negative aspects. Mutilated bodies are sometimes found in Africa with organs removed—presumably for use in magical spells. Recently, three Angolans were jailed in England for the torture of an eight-year-old girl whom they accused of being a possessed Witch.

Monday

Tuesday

Wednesday

Thursday

Friday

Saturday

Sunday

March 2007

March 1   ♃

Matronalia (Roman)
Waxing Moon
Color: Purple

Moon Sign: Leo
Moon Phase: Second Quarter

March 2   ♀

St. Chad's Day (English)
Waxing Moon
Color: White

Moon Sign: Leo
Moon Phase: Second Quarter
Moon enters Virgo 4:32 pm

March 3   ♄

Doll Festival (Japanese)
Waxing Moon
Color: Blue

Moon Sign: Virgo
Moon Phase: Full Moon 6:17 pm

March 4   ☉

St. Casimir's Day (Polish) · Purim
Waning Moon
Color: Gold

Moon Sign: Virgo
Moon Phase: Third Quarter

March 5

☽

Isis Festival (Roman)
Waning Moon
Color: Lavender

Moon Sign: Virgo
Moon Phase: Third Quarter
Moon enters Libra 4:25 am

March 6

♂

Alamo Day
Waning Moon
Color: White

Moon Sign: Libra
Moon Phase: Third Quarter

March 7

☿

Juarez Day (Mexican)
Waning Moon
Color: Yellow

Moon Sign: Libra
Moon Phase: Third Quarter
Moon enters Scorpio 5:16 pm

March 8

♃

International Women's Day
Waning Moon
Color: Crimson

Moon Sign: Scorpio
Moon Phase: Third Quarter

March 9

♀

Forty Saints' Day
Waning Moon
Color: Purple

Moon Sign: Scorpio
Moon Phase: Third Quarter

March 10

♄

Tibet Day
Waning Moon
Color: Black

Moon Sign: Scorpio
Moon Phase: Third Quarter
Moon enters Sagittarius 5:37 am

March 11

☉

Daylight Saving Time begins
Waning Moon
Color: Orange

Moon Sign: Sagittarius
Moon Phase: Fourth Quarter 11:54 pm

March 12

Receiving the Water (Buddhist)
Waning Moon
Color: Silver

☽

Moon Sign: Sagittarius
Moon Phase: Fourth Quarter
Moon enters Capricorn 4:34 pm

March 13

Purification Feast (Balinese)
Waning Moon
Color: Scarlet

♂

Moon Sign: Capricorn
Moon Phase: Fourth Quarter

March 14

Mamuralia (Roman)
Waning Moon
Color: Brown

☿

Moon Sign: Capricorn
Moon Phase: Fourth Quarter
Moon enters Aquarius 10:52 pm

March 15

Phallus Festival (Japanese)
Waning Moon
Color: White

♃

Moon Sign: Aquarius
Moon Phase: Fourth Quarter

March 16

St. Urho's Day (Finnish)
Waning Moon
Color: Coral

♀

Moon Sign: Aquarius
Moon Phase: Fourth Quarter

March 17

St. Patrick's Day
Waning Moon
Color: Brown

♄

Moon Sign: Aquarius
Moon Phase: Fourth Quarter
Moon enters Pisces 1:30 am

March 18

Sheelah's Day (Irish)
Waning Moon
Color: Yellow

☉

Moon Sign: Pisces
Moon Phase: New Moon 10:42 pm

March 19

☽

St. Joseph's Day (Sicilian)
Waxing Moon
Color: Ivory

Moon Sign: Pisces
Moon Phase: First Quarter
Moon enters Aries 1:41 am

March 20

♂

Ostara · Spring Equinox · Int'l Astrology Day
Waxing Moon
Color: Red

Moon Sign: Aries
Moon Phase: First Quarter

News Item

Pagans Protect Avebury

A group of Pagans are working to care for Avebury's stone circle and the Kennet Long Barrow. Joining with the National Trust organization, they have formed the Avebury Guardians, whose aim is to support the Trust's team of wardens who patrol the site, pick up garbage left behind by visitors, and monitor erosion. This collaboration came out of the recent Avebury Sacred Sites Forum, where issues of increased visitation and resulting stress on the site and village community were discussed.

News Item

Wiccan Parents Prohibited from Religious Expression

In late 2004, Tammie Bristol and Thomas Jones, Jr. applied for a divorce. Judge Cale J. Bradford of the Marion Superior Court granted the divorce but added an unusual provision. He decreed that they could no longer expose their nine-year-old son to their Wiccan religious beliefs. Outraged by the ruling, the parents have filed a request with an appeals court to have the restrictions overturned. They are receiving assistance from the Indiana Civil Liberties Union. "This was done without either of us requesting it and at the judge's whim," said Thomas Jones, Jr. "It is upsetting to our son that he cannot celebrate holidays with us."

Over the Cauldron

Over the Cauldron

Up-to-date Wiccan
opinions & rantings
overheard & spelled
out just for you

Wiccans & Money

by Karen Glasgow-Follett

Like me, you've probably heard someone say: "It takes money to make money." But did you ever stop to consider what this phrase really says to you?

Do the words speak of elitism and exclusion? Or do you see a circuit of energy that lies behind the words? That is, as you look closer, do you see a circuit of energy that makes the phrase, "It takes money to make money" synonymous with "It takes energy to make energy"?

MANIFESTATION BOX
budget

1. Create, cleanse, consecrate. 2. Write down "you" items. 3. Pretend.

Money represents energy, a circuit of flowing energy that continually creates your financial reality. Abiding by the universal laws of harmonious attraction, your financial reality reflects the charge that you place on the circuit of flow. The charge of this energy flow is the creation of your financial thoughts, beliefs, expectations, and subsequent actions. If you want to alter your financial reality, you will need to alter your circuit of financial energy. You will need to create a circuit of energy that honors that circuit of like energy attraction.

Unique Personal Patterns

Each person bears a unique pattern of energy circuitry. This is because each person bears unique concepts of reality, money, and the circumstances that constitute a prosperous life.

The ability of being "self-aware" and "self-true" are the first steps in altering your own circuit of attraction. Since the circuitry of financial attraction is "charged" by your thoughts, beliefs, expectations, and actions, you must be sure to look at each of these if you want to affect your current flow for the better and change your own energy circuitry.

Monthly Patterns

The most accurate indicator of how your thoughts, beliefs, expectations, and actions are serving you is to take a look at a typical month's finances. So dig out the records of how much money is coming in and how much is going out each month and take a good honest look. Based on what you see, assess before anything else the regular monthly flow of your financial circuitry.

If what you see in your monthly budget reflects a reality that makes you happy and defines your true vision of prosperity, then your circuit of attraction is serving you.

If what you see in your monthly budget reflects a reality that makes you happy and defines your true vision of prosperity, then your own financial circuit of attraction is serving you. However, if you are seeing room for improvement—more money going out, or less money coming in—then you can investigate your current circuit. You can discover and correct those thoughts, beliefs, expectations, and actions that may be constricting the flow of attraction energy.

Guided Imagery Script

The following guided imagery script is a useful tool in the assessment of your energy circuitry of attraction. Start by creating a meditative mindset for yourself.

Visualize your body surrounded by glowing energy. Focus on this energy, on the color, on the direction of flow, and on the sensation of the energy flowing with each breath that you take.

Ask that your financial circuit of energy present itself to you. Focus on any shifts that you feel in sensation as this circuit of money attraction takes the forefront in your energy field. Focus on any emotions, beliefs, or thoughts that surface along with the swirl of your financial energy. As you observe this swirl of energy, follow the circuit as it travels through you and interacts with the reality of your universe.

Follow the flow of energy as it cycles through this reality of attraction. What is the circuit of energy drawing to you? Follow the energy as it circulates around your job, your possessions, your purchases, your management of your income, and your debt. Invite the surfacing of your thoughts, emotions, and beliefs as these visual images revolve through the energy. Ask yourself: Are these energy movements and emotions flowing and comfortable? Or do you see or feel any discomfort or block in the flow of this circuit?

Focus on what your visions and your emotions are disclosing to you. What are they saying about your relationship with money? Allow the images to fade. Make note of any thoughts, beliefs, or emotions that may have induced a constriction in the flow of your energy.

Important Recharging Step

After you have made this assessment, it is important to allow yourself to acknowledge your energy constrictions, validate their existence, and begin their process of healing. While you may have noticed numerous constrictions, and you may be thinking that you are surrounded by circuitry that needs complete rewiring, you have just accomplished a significant step in the recharging of your attraction circuitry.

By virtue of your acknowledgment of the circuitry, by your validation of the constrictions, and by your intent to heal the constricting wounds, you have just switched on the power of attraction.

You have shifted the energy to creating the financial life that defines your vision of prosperity.

More Guided Visualization

Now, to continue the process of addressing the needs of your financial energy flow, again visualize that circuit of energy swirling around you and through you. Consciously turn "on" your power switch, and focus on the character of the energy flow. Allow the flow to intensify, allow the color to become more vivid, and allow the flow to signal to you that you are now initiating an energetic flow of attraction.

Since money is comprised of mere strips of paper that fill our wallet, we recognize that money is about much more. It is an energy source that is a means to an end. The end result of money is our vision of prosperity.

With your energized circuit of flow, visualize your vision of prosperity.

Visualize this reality that you are attracting down to the tangible details. Allow your energy circuit to magnetize the aspects of these tangible details. Visualize the revolving energy that is drawing to you the lifestyle and the objects that you desire. Allow the visions to fade as you choose.

Taking Physical Steps

Since you have just initiated an energy attraction, now is the time to couple the energy attraction with the physical action that will help ensure that you will draw the money to you however you desire.

Review the vision that you have just released. Allow yourself to adjust any details to meet your desires. Not only have you acted to energetically magnetize this reality to you, you have created a set of goals you can use to mark your progress.

Making a Budget

Few words can elicit such strong emotions as the word "budget." Particularly among the metaphysical community, this one word can induce nightmare visions of constraint and limitation. But budgeting has a wonderful potential to alter energy. Budgeting gives you a blueprint that allows you to track your income and outflow, tangibly assessing your complete circuit of energy flow. Budgeting allows you to see where any improvements are needed so that you can create more income or reduce the outflow of your money.

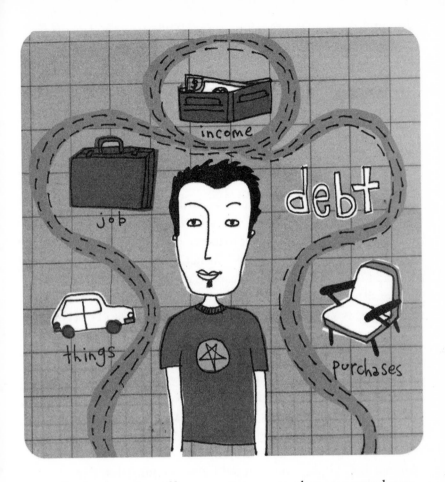

Budgeting also offers a treasure map that can reveal any "hidden money" that can be diverted toward your acquisition of one of your goals. If you create a budget, you just may find that it is a physical action that can profoundly and positively affect your energy circuit of attraction. And, if you wish, you can incorporate a magical spin to your budgeting.

To make a magical budget, simply create a manifestation box. This is a box that you build, cleanse, and consecrate as you choose. Within this box, you place all that you intend to manifest. After you have created a "now" budget, you can create a budget that is inclusive of your prosperity goals. Place this budget in your manifestation box for and wait for a magical energy punch to affect your budget.

Promoting Attraction

One of the underlying currents of the circuit of attraction is the current of allowing and acceptance. Attraction is moot if you don't allow yourself to accept the gifts that attraction will bestow. If these gifts are continually rejected, the energy of attraction fades. Allow yourself to accept. This process of acceptance begins with the process of gratitude.

> Attraction is moot if you don't allow yourself to accept the gifts that attraction bestows.

Stating at least one daily affirmation of gratitude allows you to first tune in to the positive aspects of your life. As you tune into these aspects, you actively honor the gifts of attraction. When you honor this energy, the flow becomes stronger and begins to vibrate at that higher rate of positive "like" energy attraction.

Open to the Possibilities

To further attraction energy, allow yourself to develop new beliefs; don't get stuck in a rut and remain closed to life's possibilities.

Hold a twenty dollar bill in your hand. Focus on how it feels and how you feel holding it. On a piece of paper, write down all of the things that you could buy for yourself with this twenty dollar bill. You are not limited by any boundaries; this twenty dollar bill is fully renewable.

You can spend it on one item and then spend it on another. After you have listed at least ten items you would like to purchase, review your list. How many of the items listed are items that are intended to be special to you? If you didn't include any items that are "just for you," create another list of at least five items that are only for you.

Focusing on the "for you" items, list out the emotions or beliefs that surfaced when you thought of each item. On a separate piece of paper, write out the emotions that limit your ability to accept these gifts.

Now, while focusing on the same twenty dollar bill, write down all of the beliefs that you can free-associate with money. Review your list, recopying the limiting beliefs on the same paper that bears your limiting emotions.

Hold the list of limiting beliefs and emotions in front of you. Reprogram each limiting emotion or belief with an affirmation that fosters the circuit of attraction. After you have reprogrammed these limiting concepts, dispose of them in any way that you choose.

Finally, that twenty dollar bill has one more destiny to fulfill. Take that bill, tuck it in your wallet, and go to the store. Purchase one of those "just for you" items.

Unblocking the Flow

Since you have now unblocked the flow by allowing acceptance of the possibilities, the next physical actions work to strengthen the flow and to honor the balance of the universe. In an energy sense, attraction should be in balance without flow.

Honor this balance of flow by sharing your financial gifts. That is, spend some money. Allow yourself to designate a certain amount of money per week or month to be your "balancing money." During the course of this week or month, "pretend" spend this money on as many items that you desire. At the end of your designated period, actually spend the money.

With every "pretend" episode of spending you accomplish, a stream of thought-form energy is generated and begins to accumulate. With each physical spending of the money, the accumulated balancing energy completes the attraction and outflow circuit. This completion of the circuit ensures the continuation of attraction in your circuit of energy.

As practitioners of magic, we will notice an added bonus to this recharged circuit of attraction. This bonus concerns the ease of how travel-manifestation magic can flow along this circuit. This circuit of flow can easily be energized in to a circuit of magnetic force, a force that can be used to draw a specific object or goal into your reality.

Manifesting the Circuit

Manifestation using this circuit follows the same "protocol" that you use with any work of manifestation. The primary difference is that you will be releasing a circuit of energy that is already primed with attraction energy attuned to you.

As with any magical working, decide on your intent, gather the tools that you wish to use to promote that intent. Honor the deities of your choosing and cast circle.

Visualize the object of your desire. Visualize yourself possessing the object. With this visual clearly imprinted in your mind, state these or similar words: "Circuit of force I magnetize thee." Visualize the circuit of energy surrounding the object, magnetizing it, and drawing it in to your energy.

Say: "Circuit of force, bring (name of object) promptly to me." Visualize this object being presented to you. Ground the energy as you need, and allow your mind to quiet. In accordance with the balance of energy, your quieted mind will tell you of the physical energy that you will need to extend to complete the circuit and receive your desired object. Open your circle as you choose.

Give Thanks for Abundance

We are fortunate to live in a universe of infinite divine abundance. Scarcity is merely a matter of self-imposed limitations in a universe that, in its purest sense, knows no limits. Our circuit of attraction is part of that limitless universe.

Each time we honor this energy circuit by attracting money and prosperity into our lives, we honor the gifts that the divine universe bestows upon us. We expend that energy of acceptance and appreciation that keeps us in balance with our divine source and the abundance that is our universal birthright.

Pagans and Modern Medicine

by Christopher Penczak

One of the first Neo-pagan bumper stickers I ever saw read "Witches heal." And I loved it. A friend and fellow herbalist had it on the back of her minivan.

My own practice of Witchcraft reflects that sentiment perfectly. I find Wicca a very healing path. One has to find self-healing as a part of the awakening process to the magic of nature and life. I've found the craft to be very healing emotionally and spiritually.

Through my training, I've had to face issues of low self-esteem, negative thinking, and repressed emotions and sexuality. The archetype of the Witch's Goddess, the crone of the underworld who carries the torch in the darkest of places, is a great image to emulate.

We are all torch bearers, light bearers into the darkest aspects of life—so we can all experience healing. Witchcraft is hallmarked by this shadow work. We face emotions that others would shun, because they are part of the whole. Though it wasn't always a fun process, I ultimately learned a lot about personal responsibility and liberation.

The Neo-pagan Attitude Toward Health

As a culture, the Neo-pagan community has in large part adopted a strongly positive attitude toward all levels of health. As we must embrace all aspects of our psyche, we must also embrace all factors of our health.

Trends towards holistic health are quite popular. I know they have been for me. Witches look to alternative forms of healing and maintaining health—from the more scientifically oriented health supplements and homeopathic remedies to energy healing techniques like Reiki and crystal therapy.

Ultimately, we are looking at addressing the whole person rather than just the illness. At first, I didn't realize healing was a process, and I used spell-craft to prevent myself from being ill. But this didn't address my long-term issues of health.

I used magic as many medical practitioners use medicine—to mask the symptoms. It was only later in my healing journey that I understood that healing is a process, a journey, not a goal. When you reach one plateau, you eventually climb up to another. We are constantly in a process of change. To stay the same is to grow stagnant, wither, and die.

Thankfully many of my teachers and elders showed me the blessings of change. The wheel is a Pagan symbol because we embrace change and transformation. Many Witches are very frustrated by current trends in medicine and want to be engaged in a more circular healing process. This is ultimately more healing than have our bodies treated like machines with a doctor-mechanic "fixing" us. Because I wanted to work in a system where I was engaged

We are constantly in a process of change. To stay the same is to grow stagnant, wither, and then die.

in the healing process, and I actually wanted to handle many physical illnesses with verifiable results, I eventually studied medicinal herbalism.

Herbalism and Witchcraft

Herbalism is intimately tied to the practice of witchcraft. When I started my herbal training, my first teacher explained to us that the herbalists of Europe would be considered Witches today.

As a part of my witchcraft training, I learned about the magical properties and correspondences of herbs, and not about the medicinal properties or how to made remedies you can take internally. My study of herbal medicine was initially to round out my education, but it was also intended to empower me. In the end, I had an amazing experience with herbs that changed my view of modern medicine, herbalism, and healing, and that eventually got me going on the fascinating path of alternative healing.

While working in the music business, I had pretty good health insurance and during my annual physical, my doctor called me in to discuss my blood test result. Evidently my liver enzymes were alarmingly high, and he wanted to send me for a biopsy. He first suggested that I wait a month and not have any alcohol because these enzymes could be high due to excessive drinking.

Now, I don't drink much, so I knew that wasn't the cause, but I took this month to look into holistic alternatives. I meditated on my situation and mentally "asked" my liver what the problem was. What I heard back was "fear and anger."

I later found out that in Chinese medicine the liver is called the "throne of anger," and it is thought to energetically process emotional toxins in an organism even as it physically processes chemical toxins.

Personally I didn't think I had issues with fear or anger, but I was willing to examine myself more carefully. A covenmate had suggested working with flower essences. She had done some amazing emotional healing using flower essences and thought they might help me.

Flower essences are very dilute solutions of flowers suspended in water and preserved with a tiny bit of alcohol. Each flower is said to have an energetic, or spiritual, "signature" that works on a part of the body and its corresponding chakras, emotions, thoughts, and issues.

For example, rose flower essence opens the heart to love, working through the heart chakra and its related body system. The essence practitioner put me on the flower essences of herbs traditionally used to treat the liver—including dandelion and milk thistle. These are used to treat repressed emotions such as anger and fear.

Within the first few days being on the essences, I had several experiences that concerned learning to process and healthily express my angers in a constructive way. It showed me how I had been repressing my emotions.

Though it was just a start, I returned to my doctor and found my enzymes were measurably lower. He monitored me for several months, and the liver enzymes returned to normal. I continued my flower essence treatment and therapy for almost a year until I felt I had reached a plateau and completed a level of healing.

Focusing on My Own Healing Practice

This experience changed my view of modern medicine. Although I had used magic before to banish colds and other minor illnesses, I didn't realize that I wasn't addressing the root of the issues. I didn't truly understand how my thoughts and feelings directly corresponded to the organs and various systems in my body system.

In various healing traditions, from Chinese medicine to Western astrology, mystics and practitioners know how to decode the messages the body is giving us. I eventually changed careers, lost my health insurance, and started the practice of herbalism. I used teas, tinctures, and oils to heal most of the illnesses I encountered, and when I came across something that was beyond my knowledge, I saw a local herbal consultant.

I managed to avoid having to purchase antibiotics and other prescriptions, as well as belay expensive doctor visits that were beyond my means without insurance. Only when it was necessarily did I see a traditional health care practitioner. Through exercise, diet, meditation, and herbs, I was far healthier than I had ever been.

Soon I began my own healing practice. It grew out of my work teaching people witchcraft and doing consultations with tarot cards. I learned a variety of healing techniques, including using medicinal herbalism and flower essences to energy therapies like Reiki.

I studied crystals, not only for magic but for their healing powers. I worked with astrology, specifically medical astrology and the herbal associations in astrology. I eventually became a minister, and though my healing work falls under the umbrella of spiritual, not medical counsel, my practice grew.

I envisioned myself in the role much like the village cunning man. Most people come to me when they feel that modern medicine, psychology, or religion doesn't have an answer or a path to transformation and healing.

As a result, I see people from all walks of life, from modern Neo-pagans to devout Catholics and Protestants who have no where else to turn. Sometimes my job is to help people learn techniques of empowerment. Others times, it is to help them

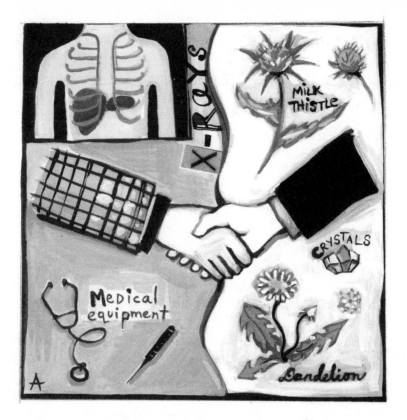

come to terms with the transition of death and to embrace the life on the other side of the veil.

Sometimes I have to tell them things they would rather not hear, or I have to listen when no one else will listen.

Hard Pill

Later in my practice, I also came to realize that it is sometimes my job to tell people to go see a doctor or psychiatrist. I didn't know that many people in the magical and Pagan world have taken their desire for holistic health as a rejection of alleopathic medicine. Many of the people I counselled would flatly refuse traditional medicine or therapy.

I had been taught that witchcraft is a middle path. We seek balance and moderation. We use whatever tools are available to us. We are practical. When we seek holism, we can't reject a major portion of thought and healing just because it doesn't always recognize "alternative" practices.

Witches are not against modern medicine, doctors, nurses, or hospitals. Although there could be a lot of improvement in these areas, these professionals have skills and talents, particularly in regard to immediate injury and critical illness that is untreatable by any spiritual healing technique.

It's simple common sense to know that if I am hit by a car, I want someone to take me to the hospital and not to a Reiki practitioner.

As holistic people, it's actually our job to look at all sides of the issue, at all treatments available, and to synthesize an overall approach that works best for us. When my clients faced serious medical issues and wanted to know what crystal would heal them, and they didn't want to discuss treatment with a doctor, I knew there was a problem.

I often have to encourage clients to partner traditional care with spiritual healing. I point out to those who are afraid of traditional health care that those who have combined the two types of health treatments have had some of the most amazing results. I've had clients who combined traditional cancer treatments with meditation, Reiki, herbs, and other holistic treatments with amazing results.

I have a client who had suffered severe abuse and went through many years of traditional psychotherapy. I insisted she continue traditional therapy as we explored soul healing through shamanic techniques, and her therapists are amazed at the improvement she has made since she began. The two forces, medicine and magic, can be partnered for greater effectiveness in healing and recovery. One does not have to be at the exclusion of the other.

Do What Works in Healing

A wise older woman in one of my classes said, "It all works." And she was right. For some, traditional medicine is the only way to heal, even though at some point spirituality might address concerns for them that medicine will not. For others, magic is the preferred method, although when they have a life-threatening situation they have to swallow the medicine, so to speak, and see a medical professional.

If you are someone who is not open to magic, then very few rituals are going to heal you. You have to be at least open to healing for the magic to work. If you are closed to traditional medicine, prescriptions are not going to do much unless you balance it with spiritual change.

In my own path, medicine opened my eyes to magical healing. If I had not needed that physical and that blood test, I would never have known about my liver enzymes. I would have had to wait until I developed liver disease, and its various outer symptoms, to know something was wrong.

As I wasn't in tune with my body, I couldn't treat an imbalance I didn't know about. So science helped me explore how my body was speaking to me and resolve the illness on an energetic level before it manifested as a physical illness, making the healing easier.

Through magic you can be more in tune with your body, although I still suggest that you undergo the occasional check-up with a health care practitioner to make sure you are seeing things clearly and not missing something important, like I was when I had liver problems.

Body Awareness Meditation

I try this meditation regularly to check in with my body. Start by getting into a comfortable space. Light a few candles and some incense. Put on some relaxing, meditative music. Sit comfortable and prepare for a little meditation. You can create sacred space if you desire, but it's not absolutely necessary. Count yourself down into a meditative state, starting with the number twelve and going back to one.

Bring your awareness to the top of your head. Scan your body, from the crown down through the trunk and eventually to the feet. Does any part of your body attract your attention? Does any part of your body need you at this time? Use your intuition, and if you are drawn to a certain place focus on that area as you continue the meditation.

Start by asking to be connected to the spirits of your body. These are the elemental and nature spirits that make up the elements of your body. Each of our organs have a consciousness to them. In fact, each of our cells have a consciousness. You are asking to get into a relationship with them.

Move through the systems and organs of the body. "Scan" your entire organism, thanking each system and organ for its good work and continued health, but then asking if it has any messages for you, or if there is anything you can do to help its overall health and balance.

Start with the skin, and move to the musculature, circulatory system, skeletal system, respiratory system, digestive system, eliminative system, reproductive system, nervous system, and glandular system. Listen to each, to see if there is a message.

Often, many body parts that are in balance will remain quiet or will simply say "thank you."

Listen to your intuition and to this body intelligence with an open heart and mind. Some people will get very detailed messages in words, images, or feelings. These might give you ideas about food or exercise, or even herbs to try. Always follow up on the intuitive messages with some practical research to make sure the course of action is right for you. If you get any messages of illness, follow it up with a visit to a health care practitioner.

When done, thank your body and all its spirits. Count yourself up from one to twelve, and return to normal consciousness. Snuff out any candles or incense you used, and write down your experiences.

As you walk the path of the Witch, learn to balance and integrate the modern and ancient, and the scientific and the spiritual. Help create a new era in our understanding of magical health.

Modern Ritual Tools

by Steven Repko

Here's a story: "As sweet breezes blow on a hot summer's day, a lamb will be slaughtered to honor the gods and feed the people. The blade used to do the deed belongs to an elder who has used it to kill and butcher on this day for years. It is said that it belonged to his father, who lovingly cared for it in the memory of his father, who used it to defend the village in a bloody battle. The battle was so furious, that the old people still recall it at the festival fires when they have gotten into a cask or two.

"With the passing of time, the blade itself took on a power of its own. It has become the sacred tool of lamb sacrifice that has the power to bring abundance and protect our people. Its power is clearly represented by symbols drawn on it by an ancestor. The symbols represent the healing of the injuries and ills of our village.

"The blade has kept us fed and safe for as long as I can remember it has never failed in it's power. It has real magic."

Here is another story: "For as long as I can remember, the farms in the valley have fed our people. Every summer we are blessed with fat, sweet melons and the grains for our bread. I told my sister that the melons are my favorite, you can let the babies eat the bread.

"One spring, the town leaders gathered to talk about leaving our valley to look for a new home. Mother and Father said they worried because the stream that feeds our wells has stopped flowing. Without water, the melons and grains will not grow, and the babies may die without bread. If something isn't done, we will have to go join up with other communities having better luck, if they'll take us.

"Up in the high hills at that time there lived an old grandmother. I remember that she had once come to my mother when my brother was very sick. She made him a tea that restored him to his usual annoying self, and my mother was pleased.

"My friends and I were also brought together. We were all about thirteen then, and our courses were new. Mother told us that we were pure woman now, and that the Mother Goddess smiled on us.

"For about two weeks we stayed with the old woman and played many games on the high hills. I was not the fastest or the biggest, and this hurt my feelings. But the Grandmother said my voice was like the music of the wind in the firelight and that my eyes shone like the stars.

"I was also the best guesser in the guessing game. I guessed that she held a black walnut in her left hand. I didn't have the heart to tell her that I had dreamed of walnuts the very night before the game.

"So it was that I was selected by the old woman to walk the fields and hills with a forked stick in search of the life's blood of my people: water. The stick was made of willow cut with a special knife. It was decorated with flowers and had pictures carved in it: the Sun and rain clouds of odd shapes and other squiggles. I smile when I remember them even now.

"I walked and walked for hours. By the time I reached the cool corner in the meadow, I was very tired and the fork was heavy in my hands. That is where I stopped walking and where the men dug a deep hole. To my surprise and the delight of everyone, they found water in the hole.

"We never did move away from this land. This water has fed our wells ever since. The melons are still my favorite, and they are as fat and sweet as ever."

So It Isn't as Simple as the Old Stories

From the time the first Witch raised burnt bone and looked to the heavens, our ancestors have used worldly objects imbibed with otherworldly properties to change the universe and enhance their lives.

As we have passed into our modern practices, however, it seems that many of us have separated ourselves from the tools of the craft. No longer do Witches fly on broom back to wondrous and far-off places for sabbats and esbats. The black-handled knife is no longer charged as an amulet with the power to aim and focus our spells of change.

Cloaks that once allowed us to pass unseen have become an outdated fashion statement, an embarrassing extension of our inability to let go of a stereotypical image of our residual Halloween selves. In the name of adulthood we have abandoned the cartoon versions of our ritual tools and lost our connection with the magical beings that forged the Excalibur of King Arthur, an

205

undefeatable sword of kings that changed the course of events in the world.

Magical Tools Today

Our magical tools are the physical proof of our ability to change destiny. Each tool requires us to understand its magical properties and be inspired by that magical action.

Athame

The athame, and its big brother the sword, is a tool of strong, commanding power. It directs energy by force of will, and through this power thought becomes action. Forged of the spirits of earth and the flames of transformation, this ritual tool holds an almost celestial quality while remaining very earthy.

In the days of covens past, this was not a weapon found under every pillow. Witches did not make weapons, blacksmiths did. Swords were expensive and they needed to be paid for in cash. In fact, at certain times, being in possession of a weapon of war was a crime punishable by prison and eventual death.

The swords and athames of a Pagan community symbolized the group's authority to organize. Back then, there was a benefactor in the group that had some secular standing. This person was not necessarily in a position of authority in the group, but her or she rather lent authority to the group in the eyes of the rest of society.

So how did we get from a weapon of destruction to a ritual tool of power? The answer: dualism.

The knife is a perfect example of the power of opposites: the power to kill provides us the power to heal. In the male aspect of the blade and the female aspect of the hand that holds it, an athame has a God side and a Goddess side separated by a fine and sharp line. It is this dualistic view of a blade that celebrates the balance of nature. It begins a circular spiritual journey from weapon to wand.

The Wand

Like the athame, the wand or staff is another tool used to direct energy. However, the wand is not a tool projecting our will, as is often imagined. Instead, it is a communing cooperation with the spirits of nature.

The material of a wand is unchanged living matter and contains the spirits of the forest and the sacred woods. The list may include oak, ash, willow, birch, vine, reed, hazel, rowan, alder, hawthorn, holly, elder, and ivy. A wand is not made by man, but it is another entity of the planet. It is an

As we have moved into our modern practice, it seems that many of us have separated ourselves from the tools of the craft.

outstretched hand or a telephone line to the heart of the natural world. Within our wand we see an opportunity to find our true place in nature and our function in it.

The Broom

Like the wand, the broom or besom instills a gentle quality of magic. Now used primarily as a cleansing tool, the broom is a symbol of new beginnings and fertility. Throughout many cultures, the broom and its more primitive ancestors were used in ritual dance and domestic blessing. Everybody had one, so everyone could participate. As an inspiration of magical journey, your broom can open new worlds to you if you let it.

Although the materials of a broom vary, a Witch's broom should have a foundation of sacred wood. It has also become traditional that the besom be a tool of protection. The end of the staff that is covered in bristles is sharpened to a point like a primitive spear. A broom hung over the door keeps away trouble, and a broom placed in the corner gets rid of unwanted visitors.

The Cup

The cup or cauldron is a manufactured form of the stream and well. It is the vessel from which divine blessings flow. Its connection to the feminine and the womb symbolizes life and birth.

And as a symbol of well and water it represents the power to maintain life.

The Cauldron

The cauldron in spirit represents divine hospitality, and as a tool of communion it makes us one and creates a community or family through the sharing of a drink or meal. Because of this quality, the cauldron has come to herald a celebration. A cauldron of some type should be present at your esbats and sabbats to generate both prosperity and good feelings.

Other Tools

Other tools of community include the shield or pentacle and the cord. The shield is an article of faith and belief. It does not have to be a pentacle, as there are many sacred and protecting symbols throughout history that can be used to represent sacred energy and divine balance.

The cord or measure is a personal tool of initiation into a group or coven. It symbolizes our connection to the group, its ideals, and its oaths. It also serves to connect us to the earth, and to ground us and provide stability.

Magically, a cord is used to bind energy and will to a focus or course and to other energies by coming in contact with other cords of other Witches.

How a cord is made and its overall properties depend on the tradition of the group. A cord usually symbolizes a graduated member of standing in the community and in some way personally represents the physical member.

Some Practices and Tool Traditions

Some group traditions claim that the only tools necessary for a ritual are the cord, shield, and cup. This is perhaps because these tools bind us to community.

But let's face it, along with this list we must also remember censers and thuribles for smudging and burning, the scourge that represents the discipline of our gods, and a myriad of candle-holders, snuffers, and various types of magical gadgets ad infinitum.

The average modern Wiccan ritual tool experience begins in a New Age shop with a laundry list. The items in such a shop, as they are born, hold little more than a glimmer of what they are to become in your possession. Modern purveyors do not always know what needs to be done to bridge the magical gap (that is, to imbue store-bought items with energy and intent).

Every item used as a tool of worship and magic requires a preparation for that purpose. This preparation can be both long and short term. If we look at a tool as a writing slate of focus, then we see the first process of tool-craft is wiping away the history that we do not wish to retain.

Please note that I did not say you should wash a tool till it's sterile. The evolution of a tool is a slow one. Removing everything that has come before can create a very empty glass, and such a vessel will not yield much power at all. We need to exercise the patience necessary to build properly empowered tools. Some of this patience needs to be applied in the cleansing process to keep us from throwing the baby out with the bath water.

Now that we have created a ritual canvas for our tool, the time has come to paint the background. The first and foremost thing our tool should be is "our tool." This is traditionally accomplished with a few drops of serum concealed within the tool's construction. The second step is to connect your tool to all of nature through a connection with the elements.

That is, your tools should be charged with air, earth, water, and fire. This can be as simple as building an altar at home that includes each element or as complex as a series of elemental rituals. Evoke the wind of a storm, a balefire, a running stream, a mountain top. Remember, like everything else in life you get out of it what you put into it.

The next step in our mystic building-block process is to include the representation of the divine, the gods and goddesses.

This can be done through solar and lunar ritual exposures. My personal favorite has always been to capture eclipse energies because of their auspicious mystic natures.

Now that we have spiritually charged our tools, there is one more step to completion. Like everything in our practice, a physical validation is recommended. Throughout Wicca and the many pagan paths of Witchcraft, there are symbols that represent empowerment. This includes symbols for the gods and goddesses, the elements, the zodiac symbols of initiation, and magical alphabets. Using such symbols we can literally spell out anything we wish to convey as we raise this tool to the sky.

These letters and symbols can be inscribed on the handle or the blade, and they can be permanently etched or temporarily affixed. The latter can be accomplished with a new ritual tool: the china marker or grease pencil. This tool can be used not only to recount and renew the charging of our athame but it also allows us the freedom to add temporary aspects of the working at hand. We can record the specific names of a deity, our names, the group's name, elementals, herbal and astrological correspondences, planetary tables, intentions, and incantations—the list is as endless as our universe.

The Bag of Tricks

When I was a young Witch I found a unique ritual tool that worked quite well for me. Much like a shaman or metaphysical Felix the Cat, I compiled a "bag of tricks." This small bag contained everything needed in my magical and ritual practice. No matter where I was, my medicine bag went with me.

As to what I had in my bag, the collection started with my fortune telling cards. I was known to give readings at the drop of a hat to anyone who would ask. As time went on, the bag contained a ritual knife, incense matches (because they were both), a crystal ball, a candle, a small offering plate, and a pentacle. Many of the items were hand-made out of necessity, as there was no local New Age shop then. The final version of my bag of tricks even included some collected herbal materials, wild-crafted flowers, plants, oils, stones, and such.

I know many people who carry such a bag today, to the delight of anyone who has forgotten something they needed for a public ritual.

Another useful tool for the bag has come of late. I have found deity statue refrigerator magnets a valuable addition for use during hospital visits. These compact representations of the Pagan divine can bring the support of faith to a difficult and sometimes uncomfortable hospital stay. Many popular gods and goddesses now come in mini or magnet form.

The rewards of incorporating tools in your rituals are reaped in an expanded sense of spiritual inspiration. I hope I have brought you some new and useful ideas about these tools.

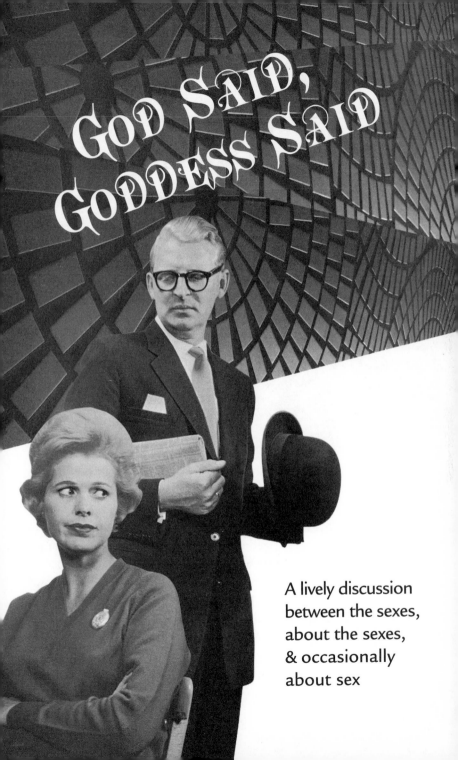

GOD SAID, GODDESS SAID

A lively discussion
between the sexes,
about the sexes,
& occasionally
about sex

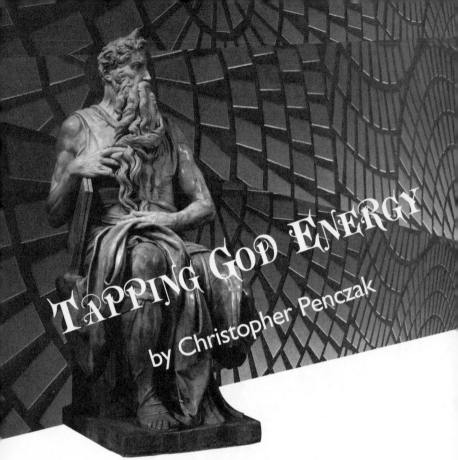

TAPPING GOD ENERGY

by Christopher Penczak

Here's a popular slogan these days in the the Pagan community: "The Goddess is alive, and magic is afoot."

Goddess reverence is often emphasized in modern Paganism and Witchcraft, and its certainly appropriate, as she has been ignored for at least the last two thousand years in the Western world. Yet some people, in their zeal for the Goddess, forget about the God, the male aspect of creation, who is just as important, and needed, among the growing number of practitioners of the craft.

An Emphasis on the Goddess

Witchcraft emphasizes the Goddess because many of us are coming from a background where we are seeking something different from the patriarchal father god of many mainstream religions. I know I was when I first began traveling my personal path into Paganism and magic.

After twelve years of Catholic school, I was ready for something different. To find a tradition that emphasized the feminine was a refreshing change. Though I was taught, by my first instructors to this new ancient path, that the creator—the divine mind or great spirit—was both male and female, instead of the default masculine pronoun we used "she" and believed that the very first manifestation of deity was the Goddess, and not the God.

The Goddess then gave birth to the God and the rest of creation. In the arts and science of Witchcraft, intuition was given as much validity as logic, and emotion held as much power as thought. The desire to find value in what was considered the feminine skills and mysteries was appealing to me, because focusing on the more masculine-oriented world, both socially and spiritually, was no longer fulfilling. I found fulfillment in the ideas of Paganism.

Working with the Goddess in some ways was a rebellion and rejection of all I learned. I had never even considered using the feminine pronoun to indicate the divine, because no one entertained such thoughts in Catholic school.

The ancient mythology I knew seemed like made-up stories, not religion. So finding something that was alien to my upbringing, which didn't ignite my spirituality, was an incentive.

What I've found in the past is that the Goddess is real and visceral and on Earth. She is the Earth manifest. She is not distant or separate from me. She understands my hopes and desires, my needs and my fears.

She is everything, light and dark, that I am, and she is present everywhere.

History of the Patriarchy

Many of us, in our initial training in witchcraft, are tantalized with our notions of "history"—the events that occurred before the rise of the patriarchy, where we envision a peaceful, enlightened Goddess culture in the Stone Age.

Before the rise of the sky and war gods, we lived in harmony with the natural world. Women were leaders, healers, and spiritualists as often, if not more often, than men. These women are our ancient Witch sisters and ancestors in the craft. They worshiped the goddess of the earth and left many fertility statues of her that we have found and honor today, including such as the Venus of Willendorf.

We look at the ancient world as matriarchal. Scholars often disagree with such idealistic images, and even many Pagans now also disagree—since we really don't know that much about Stone Age people and how they lived. However, there is as much evidence for a Pagan utopia as there is against it. We simply don't know, because there is little left and much of our understanding is speculative.

> We believed that the very first manifestation of deity was the Goddess, and not the God; the Goddess gave birth to the God and the rest of all creation.

Still, the idea sounds good. I want to believe it. It's a great idea.

Strangely, many in the traditional and hereditary craft traditions would find this emphasis on the Goddess alone to be an alien modern concept. Old World traditions emphasize the horned god as much as, if not more than, any goddess figure, and men, as much as women, have a primary role in traditional magic and ritual.

Many of our controversial founding figures of the modern craft movement were men, though some would say that these men were merely the ones able to claim the glory and seek the public stage, and the true wise ones, women in particular, stayed hidden in the shadows.

Personal Goddess Orientation

Most of my spiritual investigations for many years was Goddess oriented. My strongest guides and guardians were goddesses. The spirits I went to when I needed healing and guidance were goddesses. Most of my spells were oriented around goddesses.

In particular, I favored the warrior goddess of the Celts, such as the Morrigan. Although the rituals I learned were balanced, calling upon both Goddess and God, I was not balanced.

Though I was calling upon the God, I didn't spend much time in a personal connection with the God. I didn't research many Pagan gods and know their stories unless they related to the Goddess I was studying at the time.

Though I lit a black candle for the Goddess and a white candle for the God in my magic circle rituals, I didn't think too much about what the white candle represented. I still thought of the God as the patriarchal figure of the Bible and wanted nothing to do with it.

Yes, I knew he must be honored as a part of the craft, but I had the Goddess now! What else did I need?

This lack of balance manifested itself in my life. As a man in the craft, I had to learn more about healthily expressing my masculine energies in all areas of my life, including my spirituality. By separating myself from the divine masculine, I was separate from my own male energy. I needed to find ways of seeing the God, and seeing him powerful, yet not overbearing. I needed to see him as a partner of the Goddess, who honored her without being subservient.

Many look at Wicca as strictly a Goddess tradition, and many covens have a high priestess in charge, with a high priest who is merely her assistant. That was not the tradition I learned. In group ritual, we learned that both high priestess and high priest lead the group, but they each have different, yet complementary function.

Solitary ritual was emphasized and when performing a ritual alone, you act as both the high priestess and high priest. One hand holds the blade and one hand hold the chalice. You must be balanced in your male and female energies to bring the two together in the ritual within yourself. Only through this merger can you perform the most successful, the most spiritual forms of magic. You use this sacred merger to power all your spells, from simple candle spells to elaborate rituals. I knew this intellectually, but was challenged to properly execute it, and bring its lessons into my daily life.

Balancing with the God

By divine providence, I was asked to lead public rituals for the sabbats in a bookstore in the Boston area. Only in trying to present the wheel of the year rituals to a community that was not familiar with the traditions I trained in did I venture out to explore other thoughts and myths for the sabbats.

What I soon realized was how God-oriented they were. Not that I didn't intellectually understand the cycle of the Sun and how many Pagans associate the Sun with the masculine, but in leading these rituals, unlike Moon rituals, I had to mediate the forces of the God and get in tune with my inner, changing God

219

as the seasons changed. I found it quite difficult, but very rewarding in the end.

The Wheel of the Year Revisited

Here's a run-down of what I came to understand after I studied the wheel of the year. The story of the wheel of the year is really the story of the God. The Goddess is the eternal power in the mythos. Though we see her transform in the cycle of the Moon, as the earth she is the solid bedrock of the planet. She is the planet, Mother Gaia. It is the God who changes form as the wheel turns.

At Yule, the God is reborn as the Sun king. Like the child in the Sun tarot card, he is triumphant and joyous, ushering in the waxing year—even though it is still winter.

Day by day, as the days wax and grow, the God grows stronger and bigger. At Imbolc, his light begins to awaken the mother from her post-labor rest. She prepares for her own transformation and rebirth, and she moves from crone to maiden again.

At Ostara, she rises from the underworld to assume her role as spring maiden and goddess of flowers and green. The God is now growing in power, and eventually his light enters the foliage and he manifests as the Green Man or Jack of the Green.

On Beltane, the two consummate their relationship sexually, ensuring the fertility of the land and his eventual rebirth.

At Midsummer, they assume their adult roles as king and queen of the land. On this day when the shadow is the longest, the good god must face his shadow and is defeated by the growing dark. The dark king, often associated as the underworld god or horned god, rules for six months. On the harvest of Lammas, the god of light and grain is sacrificed and his spirit is sent to the underworld.

The horned god rules in the dark months. On Mabon, the spirit of the light god descends to the underworld, and the Goddess mourns and weeps, withdrawing her love from the land as it withers in her sadness. On Samhain she too returns to the underworld, to the between places, to give birth to the new god. The horned god rules the earth in these dark months as the master of the wild hunt and the father and protector. Then at Yule we begin again.

The Many Faces of the God

In the wheel, the God has many faces—primarily of light and dark. The light god manifests as the solar child, the Green Man, the sovereign king, the grain god, and the sacrificed god. The dark god manifests as the shadow, the dark knight, the horned god, and the underworld king.

The Witches' God has many faces. To some he is the sky father, like Zeus or Tar-ranis. To others he is the solar figure, such as Apollo, Balder, Sham-mash, or Lugh.

Between the light and dark gods are the trickster gods, the magicians and sages, like Hermes, Thoth, and Odin. Sometimes

Only in trying to present wheel of the year rituals to a community that was not familiar with the traditions I trained in did I venture out to explore other myths for the sabbats.

he is a creator and smith god, like Vulcan, or a warrior, like Mars, Thor, or Nuada. Sacrificed gods, dead and resurrected, are popular, and include Osiris, Dionysus, and Tammuz. The resurrected figures usually have grain or solar attributes as well.

For many, the favored figure is the horned god, such as stag-horned Cernunnos. The Greek Pan has been adopted as the Witch's God by many, for Pan is translated by some as "all," meaning that he is the spirit of life, of everything, everywhere. I love this view of Pan. He is the great "all" father of Witches and life, but he manifests in many myths as a simple goat-horned satyr and a lover of music, sex, and wine. He is manifested in the green world as nature, and in the animal world as the desire to reproduce and find pleasure. His pipes play the seven notes of the music of the spheres—one tone for each the Sun, Moon,

Mercury, Venus, Mars, Jupiter, and Saturn. In his name is the root of our word "panic," meaning that he also has a dark side and must be respected.

The God of the Witches has many faces, and many powers, all of which complement the Goddess.

Finding the God Meditation

Start this meditation to find the God by getting into a comfortable space. Light a few candles and incense. Put on some relaxing, meditative music. Sit comfortably, and prepare for a little meditation. You can create sacred space if you desire, but it's not necessary. Count yourself down into a meditative state, starting with the number twelve and going back to one.

In your mind's eye, see a great tree, the largest tree you have ever seen. Perhaps it is oak, ash, or thorn. Perhaps it is pine or willow. See this great, universal tree, the world tree.

Imagine standing before the tree. Feel the earth beneath your feet. Smell the soil. Hear the wind rush through the branches. Reach out and feel the bark of the tree. See the tree. Feel the tree. Know the tree.

Walk around the base of the roots of this great world tree, and in the massive roots, look for a cave, cavern, or tunnel that leads into the tree, into the land before, into the underworld. Enter the tunnel. As you walk, run your hand against the moist soil. Feel the roots in the soil. Go deeper, feeling the soil grow dryer and more solid, like stone. Walk down this stone tunnel and find the light at the end.

Enter the light at the end of the tunnel and find yourself in the underworld, a vast primordial forest or jungle filled with the primal powers of creation. Before you, barely visible, you see a pathway into the forest. Go and follow the path. Take notice of the plants and animals you see. They may become allies for you in later adventures. Go into the woods.

In the distance, you find a clearing where a figure sits cross-legged on the ground. This is the Great God of the Witches, in one of his many forms. Approach the God with respect. Introduce yourself. Listen to him with an open mind and heart. What does he say or do?

Ask yourself any questions you have of the God. Ask any questions you have about understanding male energy in your life and in spirituality. Know that he is available to you and can manifest as the kind, loving father, the giver of life in the waxing year and the protector from darkness in the waning year. He is here to guide you.

When done, thank the God and say your farewells. He might give you a gift or symbol as a token of his power and a method for you to contact him at any time. If he gives you such a gift, or even if he doesn't, reach into your own heart and pull out an offering. Your offering will take the shape of something that has meaning to you. Open your hand and look at your offering before you give it to the God, but then give it with an open heart.

Follow the path back the way you came. Walk out through the forest and back to the tunnel. Climb the tunnel of stone and soil until you reach the light of the middle world, at the base of the tree trunk. Come out and thank the tree for this journey. Step back from the tree and let it fade from your mind. Count back up from one to twelve, returning to the waking world and grounding yourself as needed.

If you feel lightheaded, imagine your feet are like the roots of a great tree, digging deep into the earth to anchor you. Record your impressions in a journal or notebook, because they will often dissolve away in your memory like a dream.

Find Balance with the God

As many traditions focus on the Goddess, I urge you to make sure you are balanced with the energy of the God. Some traditions believe in a reversal of polarities on the spiritual planes. Priestesses will hold the athame or wand even though it is a symbol of the projective masculine force, believing they wield that force on the inner planes, while the priest will hold the receptive chalice. Likewise, many believe the best medium for the feminine mysteries have been priests, while the proponents of the masculine forces are best left to priestesses.

Perhaps that is why many responsible for the Goddess revival, intentionally or otherwise, were men, such as Gerald Gardner and Alex Sanders. Regardless of your genetic gender, seek to balance both the masculine and feminine, God and Goddess, in your life and practice.

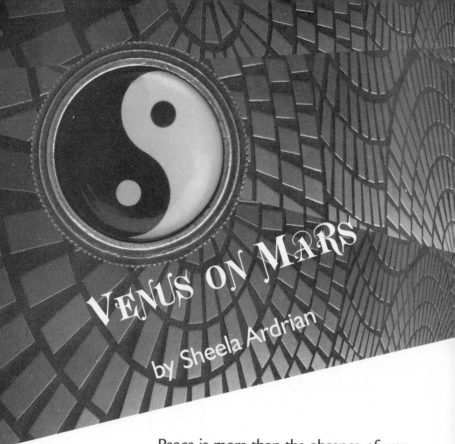

VENUS ON MARS
by Sheela Ardrian

Peace is more than the absence of war. Nowhere is this more true than in the ancient, legendary battle between the sexes. Most Pagan paths follow the example of nature, balancing masculine and feminine aspects; a few specialize in one or the other. Yet before we can understand the divine, we must learn to understand each other.

A Menagerie of Pagan Men

Pagan men come in many flavors, each with their own ups and downs. Here a few of the more common flavors that you may find in your Pagan travels.

Bacchanal Boy

He hangs out in Pagan space primarily to party, but his interest lies more in fermented beverages than in feminine charms. He gets along well with maidens who fancy themselves maenads. Young Bacchanals can make it impossible to sleep as they carouse around camp; as they mature, some turn into masters of home brewing.

Dashing Cavalier

Who says chivalry is dead? Some guys seem to wander around in search of opportunities to help out. They jump in when your tent pole snaps or the wind snatches your notepaper out of your hands. For women who have too much experience with useless men, the dashing cavaliers offer lessons in teamwork, gallantry, and friendship.

Fairy Fellow

Seen alone or with a boyfriend on each arm, he reminds us that up to about 10 percent of the population is homosexual. Some fairy fellows are shy, but often these are the most gregarious and friendly men at gatherings. They tend to relate well to women because the sexual tension isn't there, much as with everybody's favorite brother.

Family Man

Not all Pagan men are single. Many are intensely devoted to their wives and children. The family man provides an example of love and community.

Lord of the Pants

Some people seem to attend Pagan events to show off their nifty ritual clothes. This man is the natural companion of the stitch witch, who happily admires his leather breeches while he admires her hand-embroidered robes. They can create a distraction during serious work, but if you need vestments, they're handy folks to know.

Priest of Pan

This fellow sweeps a path through festivals and smaller gatherings, always on the lookout for female companionship. Though often handsome, his high energy gives him appeal even if he has a homely face. He can break hearts if mistaken for a potential mate, but he can help his partners shed their sexual baggage and get in touch with their bodies.

Questing Squire

Here is a young man who aspires to leadership. He doesn't know exactly what he's doing yet, but he knows where he wants to go and attaches himself to an experienced leader as support crew. To a priestess, he can be an asset or an aggravation, and often both.

Wise Old Wizard

He may be an experienced forty or a well-preserved eighty; the Pagan culture has been around long enough to have true elders now. Though sometimes long-winded or pedantic, the wise old wizard holds a lot of knowledge and shares it freely with anyone ready to listen.

Archetypical Males

The descriptions above are archetypes, not stereotypes. Some of them relate to specific deities or other Pagan figures; some don't. You will meet some Pagan men who match these archetypes quite closely. Most events have at least a few of each type. Everybody recognizes them.

The categories are useful because many of them get along with others of the same kind: for example, it's often simpler to designate one part of a festival, or one sabbat of a coven's observations, for Bacchanalia than to convince the party Pagans to be quiet all the time. An it harm none, do as thou wilt.

But look around, and you'll notice that many men combine the above aspects. There are dashing cavaliers who make all their own ritual wear. There are family men who leave their children with relatives so that they and their wives can enjoy a wild weekend. There are wise old wizards who used to be freewheeling hedonists—and even some who still are! A raucous reveler may turn into a brilliant liturgist once the circle is cast; a reliable worker may lose his wits after one beer. Learn to look beneath the surface.

The mainstream culture still encourages women to be on the dependent side and men to be on the domineering side.

Men with Women

Women and men grow up in somewhat different reality tunnels. The mainstream culture still encourages women to be on the dependent side and men to be on the domineering side. But in Pagan culture, we all enjoy a much wider choice of gender expression. We encourage our women to be strong and self-sufficient and our men to be gentle and cooperative. Both tend to view the other as sex objects, which further complicates matters. With that background, how can we learn to see each other as we really are, not just as we expect others to be?

We have to be willing to meet in the middle. Neither man nor woman is an island, sufficient unto himself or herself; therefore the gods created two sexes. Each completes the other, and yet, each also contains a piece of the other, as in the yin-yang symbol. When we come together in circle, we generate power like a great circuit. If women fear men, or men disrespect women, the power short circuits itself. When women see men as magical and spiritual partners, and vice versa, we empower both ourselves and each other.

Furthermore, all of us contain a spark of divinity. The Hindu greeting *namaste* means, "The god in me greets the god in you." In the Church of All Worlds, women say to men, "Thou art God." Men say to women, "Thou art Goddess."

As women are born in the image of the Goddess (in her many guises) so men are born in the image of the God. The divine resides not just in nature, but in all living creatures, including humans.

Stop and think about that for a minute. When you flirt with a man, you flirt with God. When you make love with a man, you make love with God. So, too, when you mock or hurt a man, you do the same to God. Women who grew up with a hostile, domineering God often tend to see men in a similar way. Some women come to Paganism as a means of getting away from male deities and male humans alike. But the divine masculine is not so easily dismissed, and it's hardly fair to blame all masculine spirits for the faults of a few.

Happily, the positive expressions of manhood in Pagan traditions satisfy the needs of men and women alike. Celebrating manhood means celebrating Godhood. When women rejoice in the strength, gentleness, honor, loyalty, and passion of men, the gods, too, rejoice.

Men with Men

Because of the more tolerant atmosphere among Pagans compared to most mainstream religions, Paganism attracts a lot of bisexual and homosexual men. Most of us have suffered discrimination and are loath to inflict it on anyone else. In a community adhering to the principle that "all acts of love and pleasure are my rituals," gay Pagans blossom.

Some traditions believe that homosexuals have special gifts. They may believe that such men have two spirits instead of one, or that they have an especially strong connection to the God or the Goddess. One inescapable truth is that having an alternative sexuality makes you take a deeper look into yourself, and such self-awareness tends to lead you deeper into spiritual awareness. It's just a little harder to be oblivious to the numinous after you've already acknowledged that you differ from the ordinary in at least one significant way. Thus, many gay Pagans become priests or shamans or powerful magicians.

A circle of men raises a different flavor of energy than a circle of just women or a circle of men and women combined. One tradition popular among gay Pagans is the Faerie Faith, although plenty of heterosexual men participate as well. Like Dianic Wicca for women, the Faerie Faith often forms single-sex circles. This concentrates and refines the masculine energy. It's especially useful for men who, dissatisfied with previous models of manhood, wish to explore new and more wholesome models as represented by various Pagan gods. Here they can, for instance, learn to cooperate more than compete with other men. Some women understand and support this process; others find it exclusive and objectionable.

The Divine Masculine

To understand how women perceive Pagan men and how we come to understand them, we must also consider how we relate to our gods. Not all gods are necessarily charming, but then, not all of them need to be. Some are powerful, subtle, aggressive, compassionate, manipulative, or mystical; and we have things to learn from each of them, as manhood is a complex social construct, varying across cultures and from one individual to another.

By studying Pagan gods, women learn what kind of men they most admire and wish to associate with; we also learn how to develop the animus, the masculine aspect within a feminine soul. Likewise men learn what their options of manhood are. Whom do we admire? Whom do we gravitate to? Whom do we avoid? Whom do we wish to become? Read on to meet a few of our role models for divine masculinity.

Amun presides discreetly over the Egyptian pantheon as the great father. He created the universe. He represents power wielded with restraint, and authority without meddling.

Apollo comes as the healer, with an understanding of the body and its weaknesses. He supports both the metaphysical and practical techniques for restoring health.

Cernunnos wears antlers as a symbol of his mastery over the forest and all its denizens. He is the horned god of the hunt. From him comes all knowledge of the wilderness, and the hunting skill to provide for a family.

Krishna channels his power through two different yet related aspects, as lover and musician. According to Hindu tradition, the sound of his flute enchants women with desire. He brings joy, passion, and satisfaction. Look to this god for instruction in all romantic arts, for he is the most considerate companion—a kind of cosmic Mr. Right.

Raven teaches through laughter and pranks, for he is the trickster in Native American lore. He reminds us that grown men don't always have to be serious, but sometimes it takes a sharp peck to get someone out of a rut.

Thor inspires valor and courage as a god of heroes. He grants martial prowess to warriors. Yet this Norse god also demonstrates the appropriate use of strength, for he never preys on the weak, only fighting worthy opponents.

Thoth serves both as scholar and magician. His esoteric knowledge spans writing, spellcasting, and words of power. His chosen ones thrive in liturgy and wisdom.

Saturn dispenses justice and oversees matters of honor and obligation. He is the divine judge who keeps peace among the gods. Men who follow him become masters of solving disputes.

Conclusions

So we come full circle, understanding the divine as manifested in individual men and understanding men as they embody the divine. How do Pagan women look at Pagan men? It's a complex question, and it has a multifaceted answer. Sometimes we see partners, other times adversaries. We see lovers, heroes, wizards, leaders. No one man can be everything—and yet, manhood as a concept is infinitely complex. Each man holds the potential to be anything.

In every age and place of the world, each society must create its own patterns for manhood and womanhood. Different traits and skills lead to success in different environments. Our world has grown so complicated, our subculture so diverse, that we need all the aspects of manhood that our ancestors knew, and we need a host of new ones besides.

Pagan men today are teachers, taxi drivers, herbalists, authors, musicians, computer programmers, and the more they make of themselves, the more they encourage women to achieve beside them. They are warm, funny, capable, fierce, wise, and precious people.

How do I, personally, see Pagan men?

Thou art God.

Balancing the Female Focus

by Sharynne NicMhacha

One of the most refreshing and enticing aspects of Paganism must surely be what is often referred to as the resanctification of the divine feminine. Amazing healing, empowering, and transcendental experiences have occurred in rituals, workshops, and spiritual circles as people have increasingly come together in the last few decades to honor and connect with the feminine aspects of the sacred. This openness to female power, and the shift away from male power in Judeo-Christian and other religious traditions, is one of the trademarks of the Pagan movement.

234

The feminine divine aspect is frequently referred to as the Goddess, a mysterious and often beneficent figure who blesses us, guides us and inspires us. But who is the Goddess?

Ask a Pagan this question, and you'll receive many different answers. For some, she is earth, which certainly is conceived of in feminine form in many cultures. For others the Goddess is simply the female aspect of the universe or the divine, who is either honored along with the male aspect or receives more focus and veneration than her consort for varying reasons. Still to others she is perceived of as a sort of monotheistic Uni-Goddess who has existed since time immemorial.

The many goddesses of the world's spiritual traditions and cultures are often explained as different aspects or guises of this one Goddess.

A History of Earth-Honoring

Since most Pagans practice an earth-based or earth-honoring religion, there is little controversy in the conception of the earth as a Goddess-type figure. Similarly, since most Pagan paths strive to bring the female aspect of the divine back into focus, honoring the divine feminine (with varying degrees of prominence or veneration) seems like an act of balance, a "making up for lost time" or "bringing society and religion back into balance."

But what about a great Goddess figure who has been revered around the world in all cultures? Is this really true? And are the many and varied goddesses of the myriad and often unrelated cultures of the world all aspects of one Goddess? Or is this a new form of monotheism (one of the things many Pagans often rebel against)?

There is an underlying assumption in the second and third interpretations of the Goddess that could come under review. These interpretations assume that at some time in the past most (if not all) cultures worshiped a great Goddess who was the primary focus of their religion. Many branches of this belief also

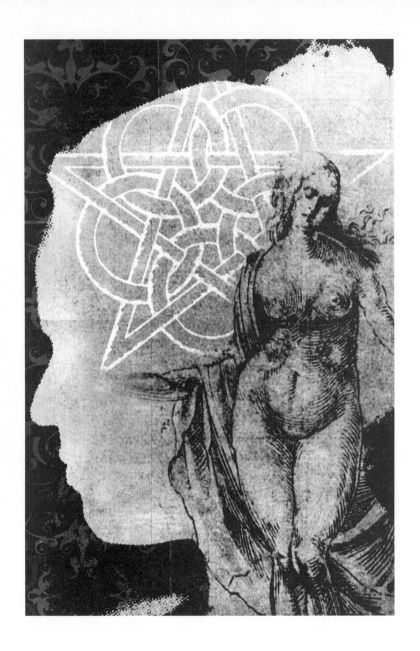

assert that people at that time lived in harmony with the earth and in peaceful, matriarchal societies. At some point, changes came into play (one assumes into all societies, if this theory does in fact apply to all cultures) that shifted the focus from female to male dominance, both in terms of religion and the structure of society.

Before examining the historical ramifications of these interpretations and their effect on Pagans and the Pagan movement, we might ask how these theories came into being. In the 1700s and 1800s, amateur antiquarians and historians (upper-class males, for the most part) began examining aspects of ancient history in their leisure time. They visited ancient sites, making drawings and positing theories about their origins and uses. They read about ancient cultures and mythologies, as these were understood in those times (certainly interpreted through culturally colored sunglasses).

> At some point, changes came into play that shifted the focus from female to male dominance, both in terms of religion and the structure of society.

Their efforts were enthusiastic and energetic, but as they were just the initial attempts at learning about such matters, their ideas were usually quite misguided. We know so much more about ancient sites and cultures nowadays, all of which is remarkably fascinating and rich in substance. And yet the work of these early privileged noblemen has persisted, most particularly in Pagan circles. Classic Pagan books and teachings still incorporate many elements of these outdated and inaccurate interpretations.

A Reaction against the Norm

Another cultural movement which arose alongside the interest in antiquities was a reaction (mostly among the upper learned classes) against certain doctrines or practices of the Christian church, and against puritanism in particular. Science, technology, and rationalism had caused people to pause and reexamine their religious beliefs and dogma. As time went on, even these new gods came under examination, and people asserted that these new societal changes were in themselves causing new problems. The Industrial Revolution provided work and "progress," but also separated families, increased reliance on monetary-based consumerism, and created a rift between humans and nature (which was now something to be conquered or tamed for human purposes).

So, in the second half the 1700s and into the 1800s, German and English poets of what we now call the Romantic Era began speculating about the "past." In their minds, this was a quite romanticized and somewhat unspecified era when people lived in harmony with the natural world and when things were a lot better than they are "now." (Sound familiar? The Greeks and the Hindus were actually saying the same thing many centuries before Christ.)

Some mythologies of the past became popular. For instance, they were perceived to represent the lost ancient wisdom of a Golden Era. The words of these poets were extremely influential, and this tradition continued well into the early decades of the twentieth century with the work of Keats, Shelley, Swinburne, and Yeats. Greco-Roman mythology in particular, followed by Egyptian and Middle Eastern mythology, served as inspiration, because these had formed part of upper class, Classically based learning. These mythologies were not necessarily embraced by the working classes or peasantry.

The work of these antiquarians and poets are some of the most influential sources which led to the creation of the Pagan movement. Early thinkers, writers, and spiritualists began to feel the need to meet and discuss these ideas, and eventually some chose to began to enact ritually what had been "done in the past" (according to early and often misguided Victorian perceptions of what that had been).

Groups like the Golden Dawn drew on many ancient traditions (which are historically interesting but often inaccurate sources) and the rest is well-known Pagan history. For a detailed account of how this all happened, see Ronald Hutton's *The Triumph of the Moon*, as well as later chapters from his *The Pagan Religions of the Ancient British Isles*. Lotte Motz has also written about the formation of Goddess theories in *The Faces of the Goddess*, as has folklorist Juliette Wood in her introduction to *The Concept of the Goddess*.

Trusting the Earth and the Mother

The focus on nature, and the interpretation of the earth as Mother Goddess (and Mother Goddess as primary religious focus) understandably found its way into the new spiritual cults. In the 1960s and 1970s, with the emergence of the feminist movement, certain aspects of these belief systems gained a great deal of steam.

These folks asked: What to do about those pesky male gods of the Greeks and other cultures? Somehow, instead of the figure-heads they undoubtedly were, they were transformed into consorts.

Archaeology also came into play, and certain early theories (which were only theories, not undisputed facts) began to circulate regarding female-shaped figurines found in very specific and limited parts of the world. Because there were no written records from these regions, it was easy to apply almost any possible interpretation to objects which contained no written clues or even symbolic clarification of their intent.

Within a decade or two, these interpretations grew with wild abandon and then were widely accepted as fact. They were then applied to virtually every society and era in world history. Despite a great deal of opposition from scholars who studied the societies, eras, and religions being reinterpreted (which showed that these theories could not be true), the shaky new theories persisted through the decades, and now they form a huge part of many Pagan theologies.

Does this mean we shouldn't honor the earth or the divine feminine? Of course not. The feminist movement was definitely

a great thing. (I come from a long line of strong-minded women who ruled the roost long before there was a movement.) Can't we just believe what we want, whatever feels good to us? Sure, as long as we keep in mind one word: respect.

If you met someone who professed to teach, say, Mayan spirituality, and you enjoyed practicing what they said for some time and then found out that this wasn't really what the Maya believed, how would you feel? You might feel angry at that teacher, and perhaps also embarrassed that you had believed what they said. No one wants to feel those things.

You might further feel disrespected. And, there of course would be the issue of disrespecting the Maya. The difficulty might also be compounded if the situation had gone on for some time, and you had taught others what you'd learned, written books or articles about these ideas, and put yourself and others on the line.

Also, if you'd experienced criticism or even rejection from others when speaking about your beliefs, your new understanding about what had happened (which caused a domino effect of untruth and lack of respect all the way around) might explain the resistance of others to your words.

If we don't respect the truth about other cultures, past or present, how can we expect others to respect our movement, our beliefs, or our culture?

Focus on Integrity

My criticisms may seem harsh, but are they so far off the mark? It is human nature to look at the world around us and see what is wrong. We reasonably look back to the past (or to modern cultures who still possess a connection to the ways of the past) for guidance, much as we'd look to an elder or learned grandparent (people we sorely lack in our culture).

Folks have been doing this for a long time, and it is one reason why indigenous cultures often conservatively hold on to their knowledge and ancestral traditions and honor their venerable elders. It is human nature to remember what was good about the past and be tempted to let what was painful or difficult slip into distant memory. In this way, we do honor the past, but we are also in danger of romanticizing or unfairly distorting it.

Most of us wouldn't delve into biochemistry or brain surgery or auto mechanics or any other specialty if we didn't have sufficient training or knowledge. Yet somehow history, mythology, and anthropology are perceived as easy enough to understand that we don't need the input of specialists.

We have taken these fields into our own hands and in playing with them unsupervised have altered the past to fit our modern needs. And when specialists in, say, Mayan culture or religion (to continue the metaphor from above) try to point out what is going on, we are not generally interested in what they have to say. We say they are too "rigid" or too "academic." Perhaps this is a valid point, as they may not practice a spiritual tradition that can provide certain insights, but, for the most part, they are also likely to be right.

Pagan Fact-Checking

How much leeway is there in having a hand in your own spirituality? Do most Pagans really have time to double-check every fact they read? Probably not, but as an example, there are growing numbers of Pagans who have come to realize that Wicca is not the old religion of Europe as was once touted, and they are trying to share their realizations with others.

These more realistic practitioners still practice Wicca but with a renewed understanding of it. Still others, in their reading and seeking, have come to realize that it is not likely (or even possible) that there was once an ancient Goddess culture or religion that was peaceful, matriarchal, and widely practiced.

Still, in some circles to speak about these things is almost tantamount to heresy.

Projecting the Past

Another tendency of human nature is to project the past onto the future. If something once was true, it can be so again. If there were once venerated wise women and healers, there can be again. If the divine feminine was once respected, it can be again.

Whether or not what "once was" is true, we are empowered (and fortunate) enough in this day and age to be whatever we envision. We don't need to project our hopes and dreams and emotional needs on to people in the past who cannot speak up to say, "Hey, we never believed that!" We must respect those elders, ancestors, or keepers of ancient wisdom enough not to put words in their mouth.

And we can surely respect ourselves and our movement enough to take responsibility for whatever we want to become in the here and now.

The Goddess for All

Is veneration of the Goddess a bad thing? No way. Whether she is the earth, the feminine aspect of the divine, or one of many

Goddess figures, she is sacred, powerful, and worthy of our deepest veneration. But does an almost dogmatic adherence to worship of the Goddess honor everyone in the Pagan movement? What about gay male Pagans? I know many who do worship the Goddess, yet others experience a real conflict when trying to interact with other Pagans due to theological and ritual elements that seem exclusive to them. I also know gay men who would be interested in Paganism but can't deal with the male/female symbolism often found in Wiccan ritual, or the predominantly Female focus in other Pagan theologies.

The same conflict is experienced by transgender people. And what about polytheists, those who worship or honor male and female gods and goddesses equally, and perceive them as separate divine entities?

Going to a ritual where only a Goddess is invoked, or where the liturgy states that all divinities are aspects of one Uni-Goddess from the distant past may not feel inclusive. This is something we need to consider, as one of the professed strengths of Paganism is its diversity and its inclusiveness.

Now to be fair, trying to hold open rituals whose language honors every possible Pagan belief is challenging, to say the least. But if we do believe ourselves to be all-honoring and all-inclusive, as well as the enlightened antithesis of the dogmas we have so often railed against, we must take the time to find out what our brothers and sisters believe and experience.

To assume we all believe the same things draws us away from one of our primary strengths—diversity. One of the main reasons we all have come to this path is so we can be ourselves, so we can freely explore all spiritual options and come to a personal path of connection with the many and varied aspects of the divine.

The next time you're at a Pagan gathering, ask your neighbors what they believe, and what path they follow. You may be surprised! The Goddess will continue to make a strong appearance, as she should, but her perceived history and her manifestations will be as varied as the many who have come to walk along the path. This is also as it should be.

While the search for truth about culture, history, and religion can be challenging, it can also bring about a deepening of experience and many amazing blessings.

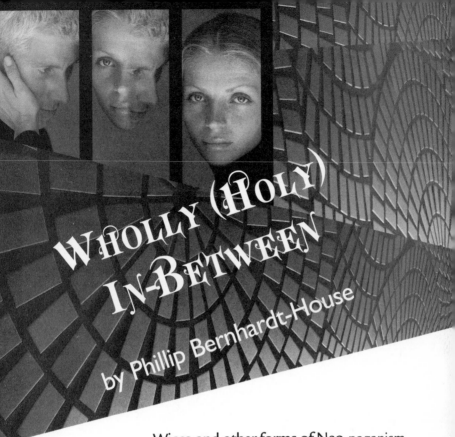

Wholly (Holy) In-Between

by Phillip Bernhardt-House

Wicca and other forms of Neo-paganism are said to be religions that embrace and celebrate difference and diversity. In the pluralistic world of today, such a thing is wonderful—and perhaps even imperative—given the wide variety of racial, cultural, and ethical viewpoints and identities encountered on a daily basis. The ways in which these religions have brought the divine feminine back into central importance has done much for creating a more egalitarian outlook among adherents and has been a great force for social change.

245

All Forms of Love and Pleasure

Enshrined in "The Charge of the Goddess" is the statement: "All forms of love and pleasure are my rituals." This has been taken in general to extend to respect for and acceptance of nonheterosexual people.

All of these notions are important and good in and of themselves. But, I often wonder if the lofty ideals of "The Charge of the Goddess" have really been fully enacted by Pagan practitioners on the ground. That is, have the ideas of the sacredness of difference and diversity once spoken by the philosophers and mystics of the Pagan movement been taken to heart by the Pagan-in-the-grove?

Have the ideas of the sacredness of difference and diversity once spoken by the philosophers and mystics of the Pagan movement been taken to heart?

A great acid test for how true these ideals might be comes about when Pagans are exposed to those of an atypical gender identity. Note: By this I do not mean transgendered or transsexual people exclusively—although these identities are often met with no little hostility in mainstream Pagan circles—but rather people who actually fall outside the gender binary entirely, either through their social role and identification, or through the physical circumstance of being intersexed.

Many Pagans know that Native American cultures recognized such intersexed people under the modern term of "two-spirited." In India this class still exists as the Hijras, and in many ancient Near Eastern and European cultures such classes of people existed often as priests—such as the Greco-Roman Galli.

In fact, most non-Western cultures have recognized and honored intersexed people in some way or other.

In Western forms of Paganism, which are generally ditheistic—a notion parallel to the common gender binary—and which often put a heterosexual act of creation at the center of their ritual and cosmology, I am not sure there is room nor true

acceptance for those who are neither sons of the god nor daughters of the goddess.

My Own Gender Experience

As I have dealt with these questions through my own experience, I feel that I have some insights into how this works on a practical level and of the potential pitfalls for people such as myself within the Pagan world. Those of us who experience this sort of life, of being a "Holy In-Between," have an intimate knowledge of what it is like to not be accorded a place in the circle that is also "Wholly In-Between."

One way that this bias against the wholly/holy in-between can work in practice is in a particular ritual custom of many Pagan groups of being skyclad. Ronald Hutton has dealt with the history and precedents of this custom in his recent *Witches, Druids, and King Arthur,* which I would recommend to anyone curious about the subject; but no matter the details of the practice, the everyday understanding of these matters is another thing entirely.

I was once at a semi-open "May Eve" ritual in North Cork, Ireland. I had many misgivings going in, but one of the major ones was over the issue of being skyclad.

The ritual was in two parts, including an open circle of a fairly formulaic nature (in which all were clothed), and then a working only for "mature initiated adepti" that was to be sky-clad. Some of the people who attended both parts of the ritual were first-timers (there were even some non-Pagans), so clearly what the definition of "mature initiated adepti" actually meant was "willing to get naked."

The presiding priest explained that the working was done skyclad "not because we believe the body is beautiful, or because we like to see people get their kit off, but because this human div-ing-suit in which we live works best when unencumbered by man-made materials."

Frankly, I had to dispute all three reasons! The body *is* beau-tiful, no matter what shape or size or gender, and celebration of this should get more attention than it usually does, if for no other reason than to counter the toxic messages of the wider popular culture about what is acceptably beautiful and what is not. If the priest had been honest and said that he does like to see people get their kit off, I think I would have trusted him more; but instead, I listened the next day to him talking about how Lady So-and-so had a beautiful ass, how such-and-such a famous high priestess had wonderful tits. In fact, I found it interesting that the majority of participants in the skyclad working just happened to be women.

On the third point, which was presented as (pseudo-)scien-tific fact and therefore an "objective" justification for the prac-tice, I can only speak from my own experience and say that the perception and transmission of energy in my body for the pur-poses of spell-working has always been indifferent to whatever material I might have been wearing (or not wearing) at the time of the working.

Needless to say, I did not take part in the skyclad working on that occasion, and, as I had no idea what its intention was and remained therefore tentative about participating in it, that was certainly for the best anyway.

There are other commonly held beliefs about being skyclad, that rituals are performed skyclad in order to demonstrate that one is "free," or in order to eliminates social distinctions between people. While either or both of these reasons might be true and may or may not have traditional precedent behind them as well, what being skyclad certainly does not eliminate is gender distinctions. In fact, I would suggest being skyclad highlights gender distinctions, and one would have to be blind or extremely unobservant to assert otherwise!

The Difficulty of Being Different-Gendered

For people of atypical genders, this situation is difficult in many ways. Since the experience of many such folks is that their core identity is at variance with their physical characteristics, and surgical intervention is not always possible, or even desired, they experience a disconnect when they are forced to work skyclad in front of others.

That is, a trans-woman who happens to have a penis might not be taken seriously as a woman when skyclad. An intersexed person who looks outwardly female but has a male genotype and personality characteristics would also find him- or herself in a difficult situation. And someone of whatever physical sex who is of a non-binary gender would be in the same boat.

Certainly covens and groups that work together regularly can reach an understanding on these matters and find something that is equitable for them. But in situations like the one above, in which supposedly all are invited and accepted, an in-between will likely be mistakenly labeled in a way that can totally undermine their confidence and self-sense in a spiritual setting that is meant to foster and encourage those things. This is difficult situation, indeed.

A survey of various world cultures clearly shows that characteristics ascribed to one or the other gender do not always match up, and they are therefore not objectively or intrinsically gendered in one way or the other. To take one obvious but minor

example, the ultra-masculine attire of Scotland, the kilt, is a skirt little different from a woman's in many other societies. In the later nineteenth and early twentieth centuries, pink was the color for baby boys (as it was thought to be assertive) and blue for girls (because it was passive and calming), but these associations changed to the complete opposite by the middle of the century. What characteristics get assigned to which gender is a relatively arbitrary process. Still, again, in many Neo-pagan groups, balances of male and female energies are needed for particular operations and rituals. Male energies are thought of as active and female as passive, or energies in general are always gendered along the common binary masculine-feminine lines.

Whether the ideas behind this are matters of quasi-science or merely of belief, they are rarely questioned. But energy in-and-of-itself does not have a gender; if anything, energy is beyond gender entirely.

Energy may have qualities that we might describe in certain ways, or create analogies to, but we must admit that any gendered notions are also our own imperfect way of attempting to define them, as opposed to making accurate and objective definitions.

The symbols on the ends of batteries that indicate which end is "positive" and which is "negative" are arbitrary notions. There is nothing inherently positive or negative about either end of the battery. So also with humans: the absence or presence of a vulva and breasts is no more indicative of the "feminine" energy of the person involved than is the plus or minus on the end of a battery.

Other Myths of Gender

When we look at other myths, we see that the gender stereotypes we employ in ritual and symbolism do not necessarily apply. A few Irish examples will suffice to demonstrate the point. The cauldron of the Túatha Dé Danann belonged not to a mother goddess figure, but to the Dagda, a superlatively male figure. Furthermore, the deadly spear called the *gae bolga* was obtained by Cú Chulainn not from his father Lugh, but from his foster-mother Scáthach. Spear-wielding women and cauldron-bearing men might be a wise thing to pay attention to in our own practices these days!

And yet the Freudian/Jungian approach built in to many Pagan ideologies would see these attributes as anomalous, rather than just saying that "sometimes a spear is just a spear" and implies nothing about a generative or phallic symbol or the "archetypal male" energy.

The concept of spiritual androgyny is often talked about as a semiperfect balance of male and female energies, and therefore something to be desired; but the concept of androgyny itself is also reflective of the gender binary bias. Nonetheless, it is about as close to gender nondualism as many people will ever be able to imagine.

It is interesting to note how the variant attitudes to mythical androgyny have existed in the East and West. In Greek myth, the "androgyne" is often depicted as Hermaphroditus, shown with female breasts and a penis in representational art. This "horizontal androgyny" still privileges the male part of the equation (the word androgyne itself puts the male term of the compound first), and reduces the feminine component to the nurturing breasts, as the female as caretaker of children, thus eliminating (in a very classical manner) the feminine, more essential contribution to reproduction.

In India, a different attitude emerges in the figure of Ardhanarishvara, the form of the combined Shiva and Shakti, who is male on the right side and female on the left. This figure is shown with one breast and always with the genitals covered—because as a "vertical androgyne," what would they look like? While this also begins to stray down the path of essentializing the right side (and therefore left-brained activities) as male and the left side (and right-brained activities) as female, nonetheless, because it privileges neither one, it approaches a balance much more closely.

What We Can Do about This

So, what can one do to begin thinking in other or alternative ways about gender and one's ritual work and practices? Here are a few suggestions.

1) Try symbolizing and/or invoking the god and goddess of your choice with an atypical attribute or ritual tool. The Dagda, in addition to his cauldron of plenty (generally cauldrons are feminine) and his club with carved features of the landscape (clubs and most weapons being masculine), was also said to possess a huge spoon, which symbolically could be either masculine or feminine.

What if Athena were invoked with a spear rather than the more stereotypically feminine shield? What if Thor were to be invoked by his drinking horn rather than the more masculine hammer? Other possibilities from other pantheons include the ship of Re or Horus (as a "vessel," boats and ships in many languages are gendered feminine), and the lance of Kali. If actual symbols or attributes don't exist in the mythologies concerned that are appropriate, use your imagination and create something that is.

2) As a variation on the Great Rite, or as a ritual itself, try working with the idea of the creation of the cosmos from the point of view of the unitary androgyne. This androgyne either splits itself into a masculine and feminine part, or through a creative masturbatory act engenders the first beings. There was a

minor tradition in Greek mythology that Atlas was a primordial androgyne who split into Hermes and Aphrodite, and the offspring of these two was Hermaphroditus, who was also called Atlantius (echoing the earlier androgyne Atlas).

Could the function of the Great Rite be replaced on occasion with a symbolic enactment of either the original split in the primordial androgyne into the first male and female as in this Greek myth, or perhaps the re-unification of the male and female into one being as with the Hindu story of Shiva and Shakti becoming Ardhanarishvara?

(3) Another minor Greek tradition concerns the seer Tiresias, who spent various stages of his life as a male and as a female before he was given his prophetic abilities, which were so powerful they continued after his death. The transformation and fluctuations between Tiresias' genders was sometimes taken as an allegory of the seasons, with spring and autumn being the male periods, and summer and winter the female.

Rather than an allegory of the seasons that involves the battle between the representations of summer and winter, use the figure of Tiresias or another sex-shifting character or set of characters (like Gwydion and Gilvaethwy in the fourth branch of the medieval Welsh *Mabinogi*) to symbolize the myth of the changing seasons as taking place in one being, rather than as a bellicose conflict.

(4) Perform a ritual in which no gendered symbols, language, or deity-forms are used at all. This can be done simply as a learning exercise, just to see how easy or difficult you find it to jettison these concepts altogether and simply interact with and experience the divine as without gender, distinction, division, or stereotyped characteristics.

Being Wholly Holy

To assume that the cosmos was gendered from the beginning, as so many Pagan practices seem to imply, is to both limit the full possible expression of the divine as well as to come dangerously close to a sort of "gender idolatry" that is ultimately not at all beneficial.

It is not necessary to get rid of all gendered language and characteristics and deity forms in all ritual purposes and occasions. However, it might do one well to question whether strongly gendered spiritual experiences and symbols are necessary at all times.

To understand how those who are not strictly male or female, but who are both wholly (and holly) in-between, experience their spirituality and the world unfolding around them is an exercise that absolutely anyone can potentially benefit from.

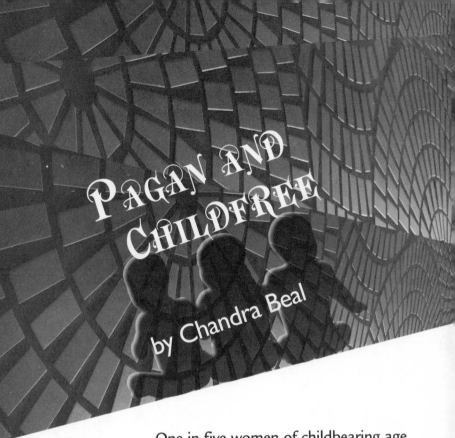

PAGAN AND CHILDFREE

by Chandra Beal

One in five women of childbearing age today will never have children, a figure double that of women born in 1945. Most of our parents and grandparents didn't question having children. It was just what you did after you got married. There was much more pressure to have children in that era, and you pitied the childless or criticized those who chose not to have kids.

Today's modern Pagans without kids prefer to call themselves "childfree," a term that reflects their sense of choice in the matter, and they reject the idea of being childless as it implies a sense of something

missing in their lives. The childfree have in fact thought long and hard about parenthood, and many have concluded, for reasons as varied as they are, that it just isn't right for them. You won't find many fence sitters among this population. They are adamantly against having children.

Reasons to Be Childfree

The reasons people choose to remain childfree range from simply not enjoying babies and small children, to concerns about affordability or the ability to parent, to just preferring the freedom of an independent lifestyle.

Some knew very early on that they never wanted to have children. They didn't like to play with dolls or baby-sit. Others decided as adults when they saw what other people having kids did to their friendships or family relationships. Their friends or family became too busy between working full time and dragging kids to their various activities to have time to socialize anymore. Some people find that when their friends become new parents, their attention turns more and more toward their children, and their common interests divide and friendships fade.

Many Pagans who follow a nature-based spiritual path take a farsighted approach to their decision, choosing not to have children as part of creating a more livable, sustainable future that brings our planet back into balance. Some believe that we have a moral obligation to leave the world in good shape for future generations and we are rapidly using up its resources by having more kids.

Society bombards us with the idea that children are a given. Our culture values children and sees them as essential to the good life as a big screen TV or a ski vacation. Kids are even seen as a status symbol, that your life is incomplete without them. Most people see children as a god-given blessing—that you are blessed to have them and pitied if you don't. Most people don't understand that remaining childless is a choice, and it is often a very good choice.

In recent decades, sweeping social changes have made people more open to a variety of life patterns, removing some of the stigma once attached to remaining childfree. But as a rule those without children are still seen as different from the norm. And if you're Pagan or Wiccan on top of that, life can become rather complicated.

Some Pagans think that parenthood should be mandatory, that reproduction is somehow a divine imperative to be valued and honored for its own sake, and that those who decide not to reproduce are somehow betraying the gods and Pagan society. Many Pagans believe, as in many other religions, that children and sexuality are sacred. Some Witches have been accused of being flawed, or that they aren't real women or real Witches, for choosing to be childfree. One woman I know left a coven because, she believed, the other members were denying her advancement because of her childfree choice.

The Strength of the Childfree

While these attitudes can be hurtful, it could be argued that childfree Pagans are even more tolerant than the average Pagan because they've suffered persecution and prejudice on both fronts—that is, both for their spiritual choices and their lifestyle choices. Many childfree Pagans concur that they don't see many people trying to understand or respect their lifestyles, while they tend not to proselytize their own views. Childfree Pagans tend to socialize within their own circles where they know they can be accepted for who they are.

Not all sacred acts entail a religion-wide obligation. Pagan peoples also consider agriculture, caring for animals, and many forms of magic as sacred. Does this mean that any Pagan who is physically able to involve himself with those things must do so, or be condemned as a traitor to the gods? Most of us would consider that attitude absurd if any pursuit other than child-rearing was involved.

To declare parenthood mandatory because of its sacredness is to invoke an unfair double standard.

Many Pagan traditions are focused on pro-creation energy, fertility rites, and the idea of how becoming a parent connects you to the Goddess/God. Childbearing and child-lessness are more pressing issues in the lives of women than men, since these ideas

Some Pagans think parenthood should be mandatory, and repro-duction is a divine imperative to be valued for its own sake.

are connected to the way women think of themselves and the way they are seen socially by others. Many childfree women report having to explain their status, as the notion of remaining child-less makes people uneasy.

In today's culture, our sense of community is based on our sense of family. When you tell people that children aren't for you, they feel you're threatening society as a whole.

Another argument goes that the Pagan cause needs more babies, that it cannot be sustained by converts alone. But even a need for more "homegrown" Pagans should not obligate every follower of the gods to produce children. Those who are both able and willing to raise families responsibly make up for those who are not.

Mandatory parenthood for Pagans could actually produce an unintended backlash against the religion. A child who grew up hearing that he was born only because the gods expected the family line to continue might well feel unwanted and blame his parents' beliefs. If the family pressures the child to raise another generation the same way, both he and any child he might have are likely to leave Paganism instead of preserving it.

This argument even contradicts the idea of parenthood as sacred. Turning human reproduction into a numbers race between faiths or nationalities might not be racist, strictly speak-ing, but it is grossly biased, irresponsible, and unethical. If expos-ing a child to a specific culture or belief system is vital to someone, let them adopt an existing baby or teach other families' children about Paganism. These solutions, at least, show respect for both families and the planet without either being compromised. Even the ancients recognized foster children as legitimate, full members of a family capable of continuing the religion and values. That should be enough for at least some Pagans who want to keep their faith alive.

Looking Down, Looking Up

Many women feel that other Pagans look down on them for being childfree, having been told that the only way to connect with the inner goddess and be a real woman is to bring a life into the world. Others feel negatively judged if they're not way into sex or sexual energy. These people feel that, if anything, parenting disconnects you from the Goddess/God as it takes time and energy away from the deity and for serving others. They find many other ways to connect with the spiritual worlds than by creating more children, and they can do those things more fully because children don't encumber them.

Whether to include children in rituals is becoming more of an issue with modern Pagan communities. Some members simply don't care to be around children, or they aren't comfortable participating in a ritual to promote anyone's fertility, while some definitely don't want to include children in rituals.

Still, events that were previously adult focused are being opened up to be more family friendly. Among some, there is a notion that children are godlike creatures, beyond objective appraisal, let alone criticism. Many parents believe everyone finds their offspring as enchanting as they do. Some feel it's politically incorrect to say that you don't really like kids and don't consider them as miniature gods walking the earth.

Most childfree Pagans don't feel at all disingenuous or inauthentic in their spirituality. They channel their creative energy endeavors other than child-rearing. You'll find many creative writers, crafters, and artists among them. Many choose to make their practices not about fertility or procreation rites but about culture and community and about relationships with the gods, the ancestors, and with each other. Some visualize the creative power of nature and the universe and funnel it into humanitarian causes or ani- 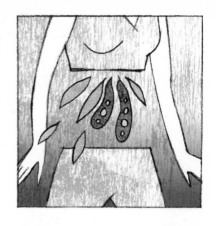 mal welfare. Others act as a kind of mother to their friends, supporting them through life's decisions.

Some would argue that because our ancestors had large families, Pagans should follow in their footsteps. Even those who consider ancestors a central part of their religion should realize that honoring them does not have to involve imitating every aspect of an ancient culture blindly. In ancient times, people needed large families to help with work on the farm or in the family business, not to mention replace people who died young. These days, most people no longer have problems with their children surviving to adult age. Because of this, the need to replace a dead son or daughter seldom arises as much as it did a millennium ago.

Few of us own farms or run businesses of our own any more. Even those who do often need to comply with child labor laws, or hire outside help to run larger operations than a single family even with many children could handle. Expecting a whole extended family to live in the same region, or to share the same skills and interests, becomes unreasonable after a certain point in this modern age. Even the ancients sent children off for fostering when they showed talent for a skill that relatives couldn't or wouldn't teach.

Overpopulation is a very real concern both locally and globally. On a larger scale, the earth does not care what nationality a newborn child might be or what religion its parents might follow; the baby is just another organism competing for resources, and the strain on those resources is already heavy.

Even within one region, overcrowding and limited resources can create hardships for families. A couple who can't find a public school close to home, or who learns that the nearest pediatrician is overbooked and won't take new patients, certainly understand the effects of overcrowding. And they might not be able to afford moving, either.

When two equally legitimate Pagan values conflict—honoring family and caring for the planet—then the decision to favor one choice over the other is a matter of personal conscience.

Fertility Is Not All There Is

There is ample evidence that fertility plays only a small part and is not the be-all and end-all of Paganism. The ancients practiced various kinds of population control, such as contraception, abortion, and infant exposure. The Icelandic law codes stated that before a couple could have permission to marry, they had to prove they had the means that would allow them to raise a family. In most ancient societies, fertility rites had more to do with the land—ensuring good crops and harvests—not the human population, which is a more modern notion and possibly a holdover from Christianity.

Deities are not one dimensional. Many people are drawn to gods by their energy and by what they embody, by aspects that they want to bring into their lives. For example, Frigga governs family and childbirth but has other skills such as spinning and weaving (major sources of income during the period when she was first worshiped) She is a strong personality, considered more a queen of creativity than a mother in the sense of having children. In this way, childfree Pagans worship the same gods but for different reasons.

Consider, both Gerald Gardner and Doreen Valiente never had children. For those who were raised Christian or whose families and friends are Christian, they often find it can actually be easier to be a childfree Pagan than a childfree Christian. Christianity advocates ideas such as "Be fruitful and multiply," 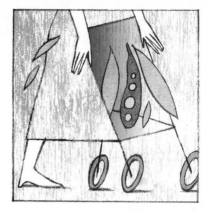 and it teaches that children are a divine gift, perhaps even more strongly than in Pagan sects. Paganism as a whole offers its members a better chance to be unique and forge their own individual path to the divine than in mainstream Christianity.

Sometimes people assume a condescending attitude toward the childless, perhaps envying them the freedom of travel, entertainment, and hobbies they enjoy. But being childfree doesn't mean total freedom. The childfree are usually the ones asked to work on holidays. Because they have no family, people assume they are available and their needs are less important.

The childfree are even disadvantaged by the tax code, which benefits married couples with dependents. Childless people help foot the bill for health insurance that is used to pay for health care for other people's children. There are no discounts for voluntarily getting a vasectomy, and many health insurance companies won't pay for birth control.

Many parents will quickly dismiss childfree people as bitter, selfish, and materialistic, claiming that they are child-haters and social misfits. But perhaps they didn't realize they had a choice too! Making sweeping generalizations about all people who decide not to have children is neither honest nor fair. All sorts of people exist on both sides of the child-rearing divide, and they should be taken case by case, rather than lumped into either a good or bad stereotype. Not every mother can raise her family to become a giant Pagan clan, and not every non-mother is a ruthless career fanatic who spends money frivolously or disrespects those who do have children.

Childfree Pagans are generally not governed by materialistic urges but have a genuine interest in the world and the people around them. Many turn their backs on parenthood for compassionate reasons, considering the world complex and unstable.

When it comes down to it, parents have children because they want them, not for the greater good of society. If they're as unselfish as they claim, why couldn't they offer a home to one of the many thousands of kids awaiting adoption?

Being a childfree Pagan can be a challenge, but there are rewards as well. One woman I know was told by a very highly respected priest in her area that he felt childless women make better priestesses. That was all the validation she needed at a time when she was questioning whether or not she belonged in the Pagan community.

Resources

No Kidding—A social club for childfree singles and couples with chapters worldwide.
www.nokidding.net

World Childfree Association—An all-volunteer non-profit organization that supports the childfree.
www.worldchildfree.org

Childfree by Choice—Childfree blogs, apparel, message board, and a list of childfree celebrities.
www.childfreebychoice.com

Virtual Witch

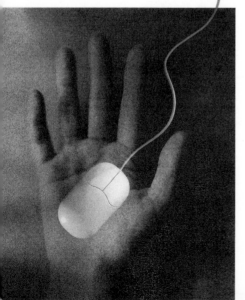

The Wicca wide web, technology, buying-selling, & electronic magic

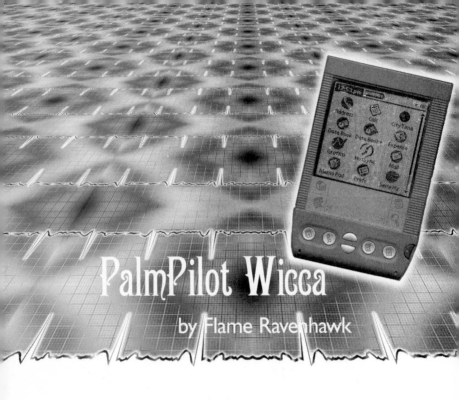

PalmPilot Wicca

by Flame Ravenhawk

Consider this scene: In a cozy coffee-house, a small group of Witches and Pagans gather for their monthly community meet up. Over the happy hum of casual conversation and laughter can be heard a tapping sound and an occasional musical electronic "beep-a-beep."

"My circle is hosting a may pole dance this Beltane," someone writes. "Will you be there? Let me beam you the date and directions." Musical beeps are heard again.

Another voice is overheard to say, "Give me a call later this week. Here, I'll beam you my number." Beep-a-beep.

"Well, hang on. The next Full Moon will be in . . ." Tap, tap, beep. "Virgo. May 23rd. 3:20 pm." Tap, beep, tap. "That's a Monday, so if you want to get together Sunday evening, we can do our Full Moon rite then."

What on earth is going on here? It feels a bit like a *Star Trek* convention, with all these people "beaming" data from devices that look like "tricorders" from the old television series. What are these little gadgets that you see more and more often these days? And why are so many spiritual folks so passionate about their modern little handheld toys?

A New Electronic Buzz

PalmPilots and other hand-held personal digital assistants (PDAs) are becoming an increasingly common sight in the modern Pagan community, and with good reason. Not only are they exceedingly good at what they were designed for, namely as a personal organizer, but they also offer a wide variety of applications for the modern Witch on the go. From astrology to tarot to Moon phases and more, these devices are proving to be an indispensable aide to anyone who appreciates the value of having such information at their fingertips.

Anyone who is familiar with desktop computers will be comfortable with PDAs.

PalmPilots and similar devices are actually small handheld computers. The device is loaded with an operating system that allows the user to run software applications. Anyone who is even generally familiar with desktop computers will be immediately comfortable with the layout and environment of a PalmPilot. Drop-down menus and "click-able" icons allow the user to find, select, and use a wide variety of software applications.

So what can this little handheld computer do? Many things. The scope of the digital device is only limited by the amount of memory it has and the kind of software you have installed on it. The variety of programs available is staggering, and much of it is available for free or inexpensive download from a variety of sites online.

How can it help you? Whatever your needs may be—in business, school, home, garden, travel, games, hobbies, fitness, and spiritual—you can probably find an application that can help. They can all be easily found online and effortlessly installed on your PDA.

Organizing Chaos

One of the primary functions of a PDA is to help keep your hectic modern life organized. PalmPilots and similar devices feature a number of standard applications to help you do just that. They have about what you might expect: a calendar to keep appointments and track important dates, a phone book for storing numbers, a note pad for storing important notes, and a "to do" list to keep you focused.

These applications are all standard and come pre-installed with the PDA. All of these applications are user friendly and easy to understand, being similar in form and function to paper organizers (the bulky three-ring leather-bound types come to mind). The advantage of the PDA is that it can hold far more data in a much more compact and easy-to-handle format. PDA devices also typically come with desktop software so you can synchronize your data between your handheld unit and your computer. Furthermore, many common popular productivity software programs such as Microsoft Outlook are compatible with PDA software, reducing paper trails and keeping life's details in order.

If you've got a busy life and many hats to wear, all of the information you store can be sorted in many different ways. If you're a student, have a family, or belong to a group of any sort, this can be invaluable time saver. You can easily create categories such as "business," "personal," "family," "school," and "Pagan," keeping all of your important information organized and at your fingertips. So, for instance, this allows you to keep your Pagan phone numbers separate from your family numbers, and it keeps your business contacts separate from your personal friends' information.

Whatever kind of information you need to keep track of, a PDA can help you group them, sort them, and find them with ease.

Pagans on the Go

Have you ever been accused of living life according to "Pagan Standard Time?" Has your life ever been so busy that an important sabbat or holiday passed you by? The datebook function on a PDA allows you to set a reminder alarm so you never have to

forget another important date or time again. You can set it to remind you weeks, days, or even minutes before an important event. What a relief for those of us with imperfect memories!

If you have a need to keep your Pagan life private, you can password protect some or all of your PDA so that curious eyes can't accidentally invade your privacy. Setting a password saves you from worrying about the safety of confidential information if your PDA were ever lost. Your personal digital assistant will remain oath-bound and won't tell your secrets. All things considered, a PDA can be a great way to keep busy lives organized.

Another wonderful feature of handheld devices is the infrared ability to send information wirelessly between devices. Called "beaming," the ability to send pieces of information to another device is what has made PDAs such a useful tool in the modern age. You can create a digital business card that lists your name and contact information, and you can send it instantly to a new friend at the touch of a button. With the ability to beam information, you never have to worry about losing an appointment date or forgetting a phone number again.

The organizational tools of a handheld device are particularly useful when working and practicing with a group of like-minded others. Whether you belong to a coven, circle, grove, or spiritual study group, a PalmPilot can help you keep track of meeting times, addresses of meeting locations (and even attach a note with directions), and phone numbers and contact information of group members. It can even help you remember that it's your turn to bring the incense. When group members create a new meeting date, they can swiftly beam the appointment directly to the calendars of their PDA-owning friends. Staying organized was never easier.

The Spiritual Assistant

So how does this modern gadget enhance a spiritual life? For one thing, becoming more organized can help relieve us from some of the frantic chaos that we sometimes find ourselves caught up in. Modern life is lived at a very fast pace. For many of us, it's a constant juggling act of demands on our time. Staying organized helps to streamline and prioritize our time, allowing us to get it all done with grace and style.

Getting organized also helps us by freeing us from the constant distraction of having too many things to remember. A PDA takes on the burden of remembering all of the pesky details that comprise the business end of our days. This frees up a lot of mental energy that can then be devoted to more productive spiritual pursuits. This is particularly helpful when trying to achieve more peaceful states of meditation.

A primary goal in many forms of meditation is to still the thoughts and quiet the mind. By letting your digital assistant do your remembering for you, you can find amazing peace of mind. Although it may seem contradictory, this modern gadget can help simplify a busy life to the point where you can carve a bit of serenity out of your busy day.

PDAs and the Practical Pagan

A PDA can assist a Pagan spiritual path in many ways. Once you've freed up some energy by getting the rest of your life more organized, you can turn your attention to more spiritual pursuits. As such, the personal digital assistant can act as a portable Book of Shadows, a celestial almanac, an intuitive guide, and a spiritual coach all in one.

My PalmPilot has become an integral part of my daily spiritual practice. In fact, I consult with my PDA each morning over a cup of coffee. First, I open my meditation timer application for a brief morning meditation. Time is precious, so the meditation timer allows me to relax in my meditation without worrying that I'll run late. Also, the soft chime of the meditation timer is far more soothing than the jarring alarm of the egg timer I used to use for this purpose.

After meditation, I open my bio-rhythm program. Bio-rhythms are our natural cyclic changes in energy. My PDA's bio-rhythm application takes my birth information and auto-matically tracks the physical, emotional, and intellectual cycles I will experience. It also allows me to check on my friends and loved ones and track their rhythms as well. Knowledge of such natural cycles of energy can help choose the best timing for important events.

Next, I give a quick check of the day's Moon phase. My PalmPilot has a nifty little program called "P-Moontool" that gives me a graphic of the current Moon, and it gives the exact times for the various Moon phases for my particular latitude and longitude.

This daily moment of touching base with the Moon helps to align me to its cycles, even when physically seeing the Moon is impossible due to poor visibility or other factors. I often work with the phases of the Moon for timing spells, magic, rituals, and celebrations. Having accurate information at my fingertips is a great help.

Next, I check in with the position of the Sun. Another handy little application called "Earth & Sun" shows me a world map of the planet and the real-time location of the Sun. It gives a wonderful visual display of the Earth in light and shadow. It is fascinating to track the shape of the shadow as the Earth orbits the Sun through the seasons.

At the solstices, the angle of the Sun is at its most extreme, leaving one of the Earth's poles completely bathed in sunlight and the other pole swallowed by darkness. At the equinox, it's easy to see the balance of day and night as the Sun sweeps across the Earth.

The "Earth & Sun" program isn't complicated, and it's a powerful way of staying connected to the seasonal cycles of the Sun. Additionally, it's also very helpful for me to check the time of day for my international friends. Rather than looking up their time zone, factoring in Daylight Saving Time and doing the math (oy!), a quick glance will tell me if it's dawn, noon, or midnight anywhere in the world.

My natal horoscope data is stored in a lovely astrology program called "Delphi." This program will track the current positions of the planets relative to your local latitude and longitude. While it does not interpret the data for you, it gives you all the data needed for a personalized astrological forecast. It even does synastry charts, which compare the combined natal data of two people.

This personalized knowledge can be helpful in all kinds of relationships. I especially like knowing exactly when phenomenon such as "Mercury retrogrades" are happening. When the movement of this planet goes retrograde (appearing to go in reverse due to the different orbital speeds of our planets), all things that are normally ruled by Mercury tend to go haywire. Mis-communications abound during Mercury retrogrades, and an accurate astrology program can give you fair warning about such times.

By far my favorite program is a PDA version of a Book of Shadows called "Pagan Resource." This program is set up like a notebook divided into nine sections. Each section has space to hold useful information such as: herbs, colors, stones, oils, runes, holidays, prayers, recipes, and amounts.

The program comes with a complete herbal reference database, but the other sections are blank to allow you to collect information as you go. If you have friends with the same program, you can easily beam information to one them. My Pagan Resource has become an incredibly handy place to store all of my Pagan-related information. My "stones" section alone now has descriptions and healing properties of over fifty different minerals. Since I'm a rock hound, it's great to have that kind of information right at my fingertips.

My PalmPilot is also a great tool for easy divination on the go. There are many programs available for nearly all of the more common forms of divination. I limit myself to only three: "The Art of Tarot," when I really need to see all the nuances of a situation; "Easy I-Ching," for when I need to see the bigger picture regarding a situation; and the "Magic 8 Ball Decision Maker," for quick glimpses.

Yes! There's even a Magic 8 Ball! Between these three programs, I'm never at a loss for a bit of insightful guidance when I have my PDA at hand.

Getting Started

You don't need to have a lot of money to take advantage of this technology revolution. In fact, although new models typically range from between $100–500 dollars, used older models can often be found quite inexpensively.

Many deals can be found on eBay and similar places, with many people selling their older models to upgrade to a newer one. I managed to get mine for less than $30. An older model does all of the things described above, which is more than plenty for me. Getting a low-cost, high-quality personal digital assistant doesn't need to break the bank.

Software is easily found in many places online. If money is an issue, you'll be surprised by how many useful freeware and inexpensive shareware applications you'll be able to find. Most of the applications I use were created as freeware. I cheer and bless such generosity!

Helpful sites to get you started are listed below. Welcome to the PDA world. Have fun!

PalmPilot Software Sources

www.palmone.com—PalmPilot's official site

www.palmgear.com—"The source for your Palm Powered™ world!"

www.freewarepalm.com—Great selection of freeware titles

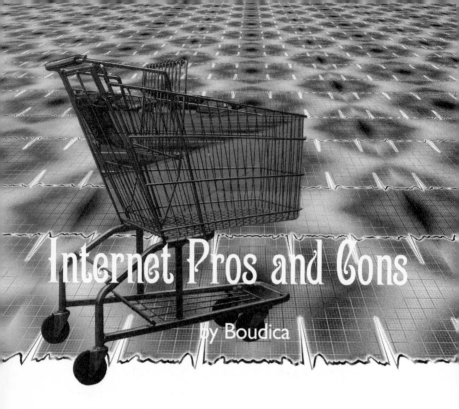

Internet Pros and Cons

by Boudica

When I became involved with the Pagan many years ago, there was an "esoteric" store in the neighborhood where I could shop and get those "hard to find" items essential to our practice. You know, special blends of incense and oils, altar items, silver jewelry, and so on.

But now that I live outside of a major city, is is hard to find such a local store. More often than not, one needs to travel to one of the larger cities to reach to a store that can fill your needs. As a result of this lacking in most rural places and small towns, growing numbers of Pagans have turned shopping online.

But just how good are the Pagan stores that are found online? Who is running them? And what about the quality of their material? Will the owners be there to back up their product if I have a problem with it or find that it is faulty in some way?

Just how good are the Pagan stores found online? Who is running them? And what about the quality of their material?

Is my shopping secure at all? Can I give them my charge card number and be assured they are not going to steal my identity?

Questions about Online Shopping

Careful consumers should have many questions about shopping on the Internet. How safe is it? Can we get refunds or make returns if the items we shop for are not what we want? Will we end up with a lemon?

There are some signs that we can learn to read that will assure us our shopping experience is secure and pleasant. We can also figure out whom we want to do business with, where we want to spend our money, and how to get the most "bang" for our buck on the Internet.

I would like to share some experiences, some information, and some advice about shopping the "Pagan Web" with you. This is in the hopes that you will help to support the Pagan community online, but at the same time that you will minimize risks to yourself. We are really a small community in comparison to the general population and there are many ways we can help to support our community.

The first issue is security. It is first and foremost on everyone's list. If we place an order on the Internet and opt to pay with check or money order by mail, we are assured our personal information is pretty secure from "cyber-invaders." But what about charge cards?

This information is stored on the computer server for the merchant and is either dumped into another computer or is retrieved and deleted off the net when the payment is made. Either way, it does remain on the computer for a while and can be stolen somewhere along the line. Or can it?

As in everything, there always remains the risk of our information being hijacked. Even when we mail a check, there is risk that it can be cashed by someone other than the intended party.

We have instruments in place with many banking institutions to assure that this can be rectified if this kind of action occurs. However, what about the Internet?

We can take precautions to assure that the chances are limited if we look at the site we are purchasing from, and we make sure the website has security measures in place.

"Secure Web Sites" use special codes and procedures to assure their customers that they are shopping as risk free as possible. In your browser, depending on which one you are using, the URL, or address, should start with "https" and show in yellow, indicating a secure website.

The "https" means the website has switched over to a "secure" location and software. Or, in the lower right-hand corner of your browser you should see a little picture or icon of a lock. The page is not secure if the lock is "unlocked." If the page is secure, you will see that the icon is in a "locked" position.

There are "pop-ups" set up in some browsers that will tell you that you are entering or leaving a secure site. You may have turned those off at some point, checking the "Do not show this message again" box. But the security protocols are in place and you should be aware of these when you shop on line.

Before you enter your credit card, always be sure you are using a "secured site." At least this way you are assured no one is copying your credit information while you are purchasing your item. This does not mean someone can't hack the website and steal your information at some point. But then again, someone can steal the records from the company without going through the Internet, and the result would be the same.

Credit card companies are very aware of this kind of thing and doing what they can to keep damage from cyber-theft to a minimum. Most credit card companies will clean up your account if your account number is stolen.

Having had an experience in the past of credit card theft outside the Internet environment, I am assured that with proper proof most credit card companies will work with you to assure bogus charges are removed from your credit history and your credit cleared up. Check the policies of your company to know what to do if this happens to you.

Purchasing Tips

So, having gone over the Internet security risks, what about purchasing from a company on the Internet?

I go to many Pagan events over the course of the summer season, and I meet vendors I find I would like to do business with even after the season is over. Some vendors have paper mailing catalogues, where you choose the item and send a check or money order and the vendor ships the items to you. You may even call them, give your credit card number, and transact all the business over the phone.

I look at the Internet as a large, always visible, and easy-to-update catalogue available 24/7. Many vendors use the Internet in this way to advertise the products they have on hand and allow you to shop at your convenience.

You can order the items by e-mail. Or the vendor has gone through the time and expense of having a secure website, a shopping cart, or has linked to a secure website and you can enter your information on that secured website, your credit card number, and the transaction takes place instantly.

As when walking into a brick-and-mortar store, you really never know what you are going to find in an Internet store. The advantage to a brick-and-mortar store, however, is that you can examine the goods. The picture on the Internet may have given the appearance that the product is larger than the one you receive. You may not receive the exact same item you saw in the picture, because hand craftsmanship does vary from individual piece to individual piece.

In a brick-and-mortar store, you can choose the piece you like, whereas with an Internet store, the store keeper chooses for you. Much like the paper catalogue, there

Credit card companies are doing what they can to keep damage from cyber-theft to a minimum.

are limitations to purchasing by mail. This is a choice you have to deal with when considering to buy by mail or Internet.

In some cases, you know the vendor because you met up with them at a festival and liked their merchandise. Or you may have visited their brick-and-mortar store and now want to do business with them over the Internet. This is the best way to get to know your vendor and is recommended. Word of mouth referrals are also very important.

But sometimes you want or need something that you have been unable to find from your regular vendor and you "google" the item and find several stores that have the item. How do you decide which one to purchase from?

First, look at the site. Is it Midsummer and the site still has Yule graphics up? Chances are this site has not been updated recently. This means the vendors are not keeping up with their Internet traffic, or have an issue with the website. Either way, it should be a red flag regarding choosing to deal with this particular vendor.

Vendors serious about their website traffic will usually post some kind of a "Last Updated" date. There will even be "New" or "Recent Additions" notes or areas where the vendors will list their newest acquisitions.

It does not matter if the site looks "professional" or not, as long as it is up to date—as you can be assured the material should be in stock and the vendors are checking their e-mail for recent inquiries and orders. How quickly a vendor answers e-mail inquiries should also be a sign as to how future business via the Internet will be handled.

Many Pagan Internet vendors cannot afford the cost of having a personal "secure" website for orders or cannot or will not deal with the coding required to run a secure website. There are many options vendors have these days.

Most common is a PayPal link. There was much controversy regarding this service when it first appeared years ago regarding how secure it was, whether it would guarantee your funding, and so on. Their policies and fees were called into account many times.

Over the years, PayPal has become one of the most secure sites for merchant financial transactions, and it has survived hacking, questioning, and the test of time. Many merchants now do a regular business with PayPal, and their association with eBay as one of its biggest customers is a testimony to its ability to keep up with the needs of the small business man as well as its ability to keep ahead of the hackers and maintain a secure base for business needs.

Nothing is foolproof, but PayPal has managed to maintain a respectable image. Some will complain about it, but overall their performance and their service is good.

When you click on this link, your web browser link should start with "https" and show yellow, or the lock should be "locked." The seller will provide you with all the information you need to complete your transaction online.

Other Services

There are other services that provide vendors with the same kind of vending ability and security when selling or purchasing online. These are private companies that specialize in providing vendors with a secure "Shopping Cart" system of purchasing for their customers.

Again, look for the yellow "Secure Site" color in the URL or the little "locked" icon on your browser. There are many of these companies, and vendor experience will determine which of these will succeed and which ones fail to provide good customer experiences. Be sure to make your vendor aware of any problems you may have with the "Shopping Cart" software. This is usually the only way the vendor knows how well the software company is working for them.

You should always check the vendors' policies regarding shipping, shipping fees, and returns. All vendors do not have the same policies, and you should read this carefully before making any purchase.

Ask: What are their shipping policies? What carrier do they ship by? What is the cost of shipping and handling?

Handling usually refers to the packing of your item when it is shipped to you. The type of item and how fragile it is will determine the additional cost of handling to you.

Return policies also vary, depending on what you are purchasing. Sometimes if the item is particularly fragile or expensive, the vendor will offer the ability for you to purchase additional insurance on the item being shipped. Always to be sure to ask about this in any case, because it is good protection to have if you can get it at a cheap price.

The Post Office and UPS have various policies on what they will or will not cover in terms of package insurance. Please check this carefully, and know that if the item is over $50 you should ask for additional insurance. The cost is minimal, but the peace of mind and the avoidance of a potentially disappointing experience may well be covered by the fifty cents or dollar additional for the insurance.

No one wants to receive a broken item, and going back to the vendor for replacement can be difficult, especially if the vendor's policy is to place liability on the buyer when the additional insurance is offered and the buyer turns it down. Please read shipping and handling policies before you buy anything online that will be mailed to you.

Overseas Shopping and Other Sites

Recently on eBay I've noticed items from overseas at some very cheap prices. While the opening bids (or the "Buy Now" prices) seem extremely cheap for the items being offered, what is outrageous is the $88, or more, shipping and handling fees being charged by the vendors.

Now, it may cost a bit more to ship from the Pacific Rim, but $88 is outrageous, in my opinion, for an item costing $25 or less. Again, always please check the shipping and handling charges very carefully before you purchase any item.

Return policies should ideally state that if you are not completely satisfied with your purchase, you can return your item for full refund. However, there are variations on that, depending on the item. Again, please read the policies carefully.

Finally, there are vendors who are doing business through some very reputable firms.

eBay and Amazon.com offer a place where Pagans can sell their wares backed up by a very reputable firm. You can find many Pagan vendors on eBay, selling both antiques as well as hand-crafted items. Many will make note of their items for sale on your local Yahoo lists.

Again, this is a trust thing. If you know the vendor, you can just find a bargain. But at the same time "word of mouth" will serve you well in many cases. Also check the "vendor ratings" very carefully.

There is a "Pagan" version of this service, called "E-Witch" (at www.e-witch.com). This service has been around since 1998 and was sold once in 2001. The service has enjoyed a good reputation in the Pagan community and is worth a visit. Again, paying attention to word-of-mouth personal experiences with the individual vendors is advised.

And finally, you should always consider the Amazon MarketPlace. Looking for good deals on books, CDs, and DVDs has always been the key feature of Amazon, but you will find Pagan book vendors in the "MarketPlace" space on this site. Here there are many Pagans offering new and used books below the pricing of Amazon.

It is worth tracking down Pagan vendors who sell through the MarketPlace, as they are backed by Amazon's guarantee of fast service and pricing. "Word of mouth" will be your guideline as well as the vendor ratings.

The Internet May Be for You

If you have a local vendor, you are lucky. Shopping for books and supplies is not a major concern for you. But if you do not have this advantage, shopping on the Internet can be an enjoyable alternative, providing a safe and pleasant experience if you follow some basic guidelines.

Again, "word of mouth" (I can't say this enough) is the best way to know what to expect from an online vendor, but following some simple observations can also make the first time experience painless and rewarding.

Supporting our own is one way we can assure that the Pagan community thrives and grows. Take the extra moment to seek out a Pagan vendor and show your support for the community you live in. There are lots of good vendors; it takes only a little bit of your time to establish a good working relationship with the best of them.

About the Authors

Sheela Ardrian writes eclectic spirituality, erotica, and alternative sexualities; her preferred style is off-the-wall and beyond the pale. Her hobbies include frightening the horses and rocking the boat. You can reach her at: SheelaArdrian@hotmail.com.

Elizabeth Barrette serves as the managing editor of *PanGaia*. She has been involved with the Pagan community for more than seventeen years. Her other writing fields include speculative fiction and gender studies. She lives in central Illinois; visit her website at: http://www.worthlink.net/~ysabet/sitemap.html.

Chandra Moira Beal is a freelance writer currently living in London, England. Chandra is Sanskrit for "the Moon." She has authored three books and published hundreds of articles, all inspired by her day-to-day adventures. Chandra is also a massage therapist and Reiki practitioner. Visit www.beal-net.com/laluna.

Phillip Bernhardt-House is one of the founding members of the Ecclesia Antinoi, a queer Graeco-Roman-Egyptian reconstructionist spirituality. In everyday life, Phillip is an academic Celticist. Phillip's website and contact information can be found at http://www.liminalityland.com/aediculaantinoi.htm.

Boudica is reviews editor and co-owner of *The Wiccan/Pagan Times* and owner of *The Zodiac Bistro,* both online publications. She is a teacher with the CroneSpeak organization, teaching both on and off the net and at many festivals and gatherings. A former New Yorker, she now resides in Ohio.

Jennifer Cobb lives in an enchanted waterfront village. She's freed up resources for what she loves: family, gardens, fitness, and fabulous food. When she's not running country roads or wandering the beach, she writes articles and a video documentary called "Disparate Places." Contact her at gaias.garden@sympatico.ca.

Emely Flak is a practicing solitary Witch from Australia. When she is not writing, she works as a learning and development professional. Much of her work is dedicated to embracing the ancient wisdom of Wicca for personal empowerment, particularly in the competitive work environment.

Karen Glasgow-Follett has been actively practicing witchcraft for thirty-three years. Karen currently teaches classes in the theory and practice of witchcraft, meditation, and developing psychic awareness. Karen lives in the Midwest with her husband and two sons.

Sharynne NicMhacha is a Canadian teacher and bard of Irish and Scottish ancestry, and a direct descendant of Clan MacLeod. She has studied Celtic languages and mythology at Harvard University, has taught at colleges in the U.S. and British Isles, and has recently published her first book.

Christopher Penczak is an eclectic Witch, author, and healing facilitator in New Hampshire. He travels the U.S. leading workshops and classes in witchcraft, meditation, and healing. Christopher is also the author of several books. For more information, visit www.christopherpenczak.com.

Diana Rajchel lives in Minneapolis and writes about everything she possibly can. She has practiced Wicca for nine years and has believed in the magic of the divine for much longer. She actually can't stand long walks on the beach with another person, and never holds hands on ice.

Flame Ravenhawk teaches and writes about topics of interest to the Pagan community. Her work has appeared in many publications. She maintains a website at www.flamesfirepit.org dedicated to the exploration of shamanic Wicca and Pagan philosophy.

Steven Repko is an elder and founding member of the Coven of NatureWise. He has studied within the craft for more than three decades. An astrologer, medium, musician, and poet, he and his wife Bonnie are owners of Gem N Aries, in Mays Landing, NJ. They provide free online shopping at http://www.gemnaries.com.

Cerridwen Iris Shea is a tarot-reading, horseracing, and ice hockey–loving former urban, currently suburban, and soon-to-be rural Witch. Her website is www.cerridwenscottage.com. This is her tenth year writing for Llewellyn's annuals.

Norman Shoaf has written hundreds of articles on topics such as church burnings in the South, suicide in France, Sinhalese-Tamil strife in Sri Lanka, the role of women in Thailand, and interfaith dialogue. His writings have earned him recognition from the California Newspaper Publishers Association, the Suburban Newspaper Association, and the American Press Institute, among other organizations. His book, *Random Epiphanies,* was published in 2005.

Tammy Sullivan is a full-time writer and solitary Witch who writes from her home in the foothills of the Great Smoky Mountains. She is the author of several books. Her work has appeared in the Llewellyn almanacs and *Circle* magazine.